"THE MYSTERY BETWEEN THE SEED OF THE WOMAN AND THE SEED OF LUCIFER, FINALLY REVEALED"

(GEN. 3:15)

Septimus Bacourt

authorHOUSE®

AuthorHouse™
1663 Liberty Drive
Bloomington, IN 47403
www.authorhouse.com
Phone: 1 (800) 839-8640

Published by AuthorHouse 09/06/2016

ISBN: 978-1-5246-2706-5 (sc)
ISBN: 978-1-5246-2707-2 (hc)
ISBN: 978-1-5246-2705-8 (e)

Library of Congress Control Number: 2016914334

Print information available on the last page.

Any people depicted in stock imagery provided by Thinkstock are models, and such images are being used for illustrative purposes only. Certain stock imagery © Thinkstock.

This book is printed on acid-free paper.

Scripture quotations marked KJV are from the Holy Bible, King James Version (authorized version) first published in 1611. Quoted from the KJV Classic Reference Bible, Copyright © 1983 by the Zondervan Corporation.

"This book revealed the mysteries,concerning the house of (Jacob),who was scattered,into the four corners of the world,religious organizations today never preached about those mysteries"

Septimus Bacourt,92 walnut st,East Hartford Ct 06108,Author

Contents

Preface

I grew up as a member of Baptist mission in the southern part of Haiti. I usually went to church with my family, but never really understood anything about the Book of Covenant. They always did the Sunday school in the New Testament, but never touched or taught the Old Testament. It took me many years until the Spirit of Truth revealed to me those mysteries. Nobody can understand the language of the prophets, the language of Yeshua and the disciples, if you do not fully understand the five books of Moses. Now there are more preachers than any time in history, but do they understand the Book of Covenant? The answer is no. The reason the Most High didn't call them is because they entered into the field for themselves. Read that in (**Jeremiah 23:16 and 21**). Those preachers could not recognize the sheep of the Most High among the Luciferian people they're mixed up with. The Book of Covenant wasn't for all nations. This covenant was for one group of people scattered among all nations in captivity. If you are not born into this bloodline, you don't need to waste your time studying this book. Read that in (**Psalm 147:19–20**). It is not for you. In my book, you will learn about two groups of people totally different living on earth. One group of people is the heritage of Elohim; the other group is the heritage of Lucifer, both living together on earth, but now the seed of Lucifer controls the whole earth—business, commerce, governments, and religions.

Read (**Maccabees 5:1–27**), quoted in the Septuagint. There you will find what the ancestors of the same group of people who control the world now did to your ancestors. You will be shaken when you read that. Not too many organizations or preachers have knowledge of what I will show you in this book, or some of them may have that knowledge but hide it, because if they preach it, members will leave the organization. Some pastors who preach others are not even from the bloodline of the good "seed."

This book is not about to make difference between race and to discriminate against anybody. It is about revealing the truth. The book will be about the difference between the house of Jacob and the other pagan nations.

Introduction

Before you read this book, you have to clean your mind from all that you already learned from religious organizations. Don't read it with you mind set up. You will never learn the ancient wisdom. This book is about to help you understand two mysteries never revealed for many centuries, because the religious leaders you listen to are set up for one thing—their wallet. They don't care about your soul. The reason why we got so many denominations in the world is because people just ignored the meaning of some of the key words in the Book of Covenant. Those words will help you reveal the mystery, because every one of them are connected to the root Hebrew alphabet of the creation. They aren't as simple as people think. If you don't understand the meaning of them, don't waste your time reading this book. Each of the twenty-two letters in the Hebrew alphabet has a different meaning for the creation, because creation came into existence with words. Anything happening in the invisible world must manifest in the physical world, because the twenty-two letters in the Hebrew alphabet connect the invisible world with the physical world. In this book, we will deal with the importance of words, because the twenty-two letters of the Hebrew alphabet are the origin of everything our eyes could or could not see. People think, by reading the Book of Covenant, it's enough to comprehend it. The only way you can understand this book is if Elohim opened your eyes. For him to open your eyes, you have to be born from his image. Put two men together, one born to the image of Elohim, the other one born to the image of heylale, or born in the flesh. You may not see any big difference. They're identical in the physical form, but interiorly, there is a big difference. The bloodline is not the same. One born to the bloodline of Elohim; the other one born to the bloodline of heylale, the serpent, or born in the flesh. These are the two groups of people living on the whole earth. This is the mystery people who read the book of the covenant didn't understand. That means salvation is only for the people who were born to the same root of bloodline of Elohim but not the bloodline of the serpent or born in the flesh. By reading the introduction, you already know the difference of the two groups of people, but don't read this booklet the same way you read other books. You have to pay attention to some key words to understand this mystery. Remember the twenty-two letters of the Hebrew alphabet are the mothers of all languages on earth.

The Seed of the Woman and the Seed of Lucifer

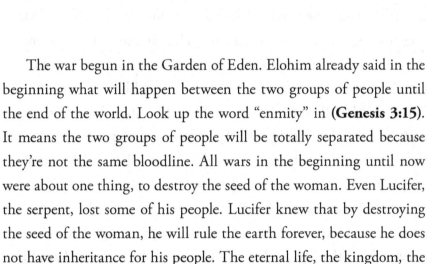

The war begun in the Garden of Eden. Elohim already said in the beginning what will happen between the two groups of people until the end of the world. Look up the word "enmity" in **(Genesis 3:15)**. It means the two groups of people will be totally separated because they're not the same bloodline. All wars in the beginning until now were about one thing, to destroy the seed of the woman. Even Lucifer, the serpent, lost some of his people. Lucifer knew that by destroying the seed of the woman, he will rule the earth forever, because he does not have inheritance for his people. The eternal life, the kingdom, the whole earth were for the seed of the woman. Lucifer ruled the earth with three key elements—empires, commerce, and religions—but at the end, the seed of the woman will rule the earth forever. The element that made major separation between the seed of the woman and the seed of the serpent Lucifer was the blood. The soul and the blood are the same. They're mixed together. The Most High knew his bloodline among the heathen. Lucifer was not in war with his bloodline, but in war with the bloodline of Yahuah.

People read the Book of Covenant, but never comprehend what happened in the world. People believed what the pastors or the evangelists told them are truth. They don't show the Most High they want to go further to learn. The pastors or the evangelists, they don't know the secret. The Most High didn't reveal that to them. The Most High revealed his secret to his servants or his prophets, the bloodline of the woman, not the bloodline of the serpent. Today there are many who preached the gospel without knowing if they are the bloodline of the dragon, the son and daughter of heylale Lucifer. Many of them are pastors, evangelists, or priests. In this booklet, I will reveal to you what the religious organizations don't preach to the members. They couldn't see into the Book of Covenant the mystery, because the Most High didn't give them the wisdom to understand that. To comprehend the mystery of the two bloodlines, you have to be called by Elohim. Let's look at the Red Cross, which was founded by Clarissa Harlowe Barton in May 21, 1881. She was behind this infernal blood machine under the title "Donate blood." Why? Just to mix up their blood with the royal blood. Lucifer knew what the Most High told Moses after his people left Egypt concerning blood. Read that for yourself in the book of (**Deuteronomy 7:2–3**). The Most High told the children of Israel not to marry with the Canaanites people. Why? There is a big secret behind that. Read that for yourself in the book of (**Ezra 9:2**). Look for the word "mingled" in that verse. The only way people could mix up together was by blood, no other way. The seed of the woman is not supposed to mingle with the seed of the serpent. Ezra knew what Yahuah told Moses before. Religious organizations preached all humans beings were created in the image of the Most High. That's not true. All human beings are not created in the image of the Most High. If all human beings are created in the image of the Most High, (**Genesis 3:15**) is not supposed to be in the Book of Covenant, because there are two seeds in that verse. "Seed" means lineage, posterity, and descendant of somebody. The reason why you never heard religious organizations preach about the two seeds is because most religious organizations were founded from the seed of Lucifer. They hide that, because they know where they came from. They also know the gospel they preach are from their father, not the Most High, the father of the good seed, because the good seed was into the captivity among the bad seed since AD 70 until now. Yahusha, the son of Yahuah, didn't die for the seed of the serpent Lucifer. Religious organizations stand behind **(John 3:16)** to show Yahusha has died for everybody, without checking **(Genesis 3:15)** to determine what world **(John 3:16)** spoke about, because there are two worlds in **(Genesis 3:15)**, the world of the good seed and the world of the bad seed. John did not make any mistake. He knew exactly what world he spoke about when he said the Most High so love the world in John 3:16. He referred to the seed of the woman in **(Genesis 3:15)**. Yahusha also spoke, in the book of John chapter 17, about the same two worlds Moses spoke about in the book of **(Genesis 3:15)**. The woman in the book of **(Genesis 3:15)** also symbolises the nation bloodline of the Most High. Let's look in the book of **(John 17:9)** the verse "I pray not for the world," meaning, the seed of the serpent in **(Genesis 3:15)**. In the same verse again, "but for them which thou hast given me, for they are thine." This is the world John spoke in **(John 3:16)**. Precept upon precept Yahusha spoke in **(John 17:9)** about the same two worlds Moses has spoken in **(Genesis 3:15)**. This is a mystery. If the Most High didn't give you wisdom, you couldn't understand that. In the book of **(John 17:20)** again, Yahusha pray for another group of people. Remember when Yahusha was born in the city of Nazareth, there were only three tribes in the city of Jerusalem—Judah, Levi, and Bajamin. The ten northern tribes were among the heathen since 721 BC. In the time of Shalmaneser, king of Assyria, they're the group of people Yahusha mentioned in his prayer in the book of **(John 17:20)**, not the heathen, the seed of the serpent Lucifer. Yahusha didn't pray for the seed of the serpent. He prayed for the seed of the woman. Because he was the posterity of the woman who shall bruise the head of the Serpent, but who crucified Yahusha? The posterity of the woman?

The Roman, the posterity of the Serpent, Lucifer, Herod, and the Roman are the same people—the descendant of Edom. They were the enemies who bruised his heel. The posterity of the Serpent must rule the world first. After that the posterity of the woman will rule the world forever. The posterity of the Serpent Lucifer will be servants, handmaids, some of them will be in captivities into the hand of the posterity of the woman forever. The posterity of the Serpent ruled Babylon from Nimrod to United Stated of America under the governance of Lucifer. After that, the posterity of the woman will rule the whole world under the governance of the Most High. Now there will be no peace upon earth, because "Babylon" means "confusion." For example, one country will be at war with another country in the same system, or sometimes people in the same country devise a fight because one group keeps all the wealth and the other group lives in poverty. Why all those things happened in the world now, let me tell you the secret. The word "confusion" didn't come from the Most High. This word took place into Lucifer after his rebellion. The Most High dismissed him in his kingdom. The real meaning of this word is "Lucifer was in war with himself." In this case, the word "confusion" was another name for Lucifer. Now let's focus upon the posterity of the woman. This group of angelic being who was born in the earth to be the ruler of the kingdom of the Most High in the last day, because, to be the ruler of the kingdom of the Most High, you must not corrupt, meaning, pure royal blood. The Book of Covenant showed clearly the real ruler of that kingdom, but Lucifer confused all human beings, by letting them understood the Most High called everybody. By doing that, he confused the descendant of the woman also, who was among the heathen. Why did he do it? There is a reason for that. He even let his on posterity know they were the people of the Most High. He did all those things for one reason—he doesn't want the posterity of the woman who was among his people know who they were. If they knew who they were, they will return to the Most High for deliverance. To keep them confused, he kept his own people confused also, because his name is confusion. Look into the world now. His posterity, Julius Caesar, the first Roman dictator, was the founder of all religions under the god name Jesus Christ. Yahusha, the son of Mary, wasn't called god the Father too. Where did that word come from? Why is the pagan word mentioned in the Book of Covenant? This word came from the Egyptian mythology, the Egyptian dog guide god head. The Hebrew language reads right to left. Read the word "god" right to left. It changes to the word "dog." In this case, the word "god" came from the English word guide, even into this day in our societies, the dog guide the blind. This is where that god name came from. That word doesn't come from the Hebrew language. Why did Lucifer inject this pagan word into the Book of Covenant? Why did he lie to his own people? Who was behind that word? Why did he confuse the whole world with the "dog guide god" head in the Egyptian mythology? When he was behind that word, all those questions are only for two reasons. First behind that word, he was that god. Second, he doesn't want the seed of the woman to know the real name of the Most High by acting this way. He won the battle over the seed of the woman. His seed and the seed of the woman also worshipped him under the symbol or god name dog. Remember, when reading the Book of the Covenant, be careful of some words. They did not come from to the original Hebrew language, but is pagan. The only way you can understand what will happen in the last day, you must understand what has happened before, because what you are waiting for in the last day already happened before. Elohim will bring back what already happened. To understand the group of nations today, you must understand each house of people into the book of Genesis and which group of nations they become today. This is the only way you can understand the secret of this covenant.

Why do I always used the word "covenant"? Covenant is a word that unites two sides. Each side has to be faithful according to what they say or what they're signing for. This is the meaning of this word.

Now let's begin with the man the house of Adam. Remember Adam was created in the image of Elohim, with the royal blood. An image isn't the real person, but the reflection of him. In this case, Adam was the reflection of Elohim. The mystery religious organizations don't understand that all human beings came from Adam, but all human beings don't carry out the image of Elohim or carry the royal blood. Let's say, for example, a mango fruit. We call all of them mango, but all mangos aren't the same. The same thing among the animals. We call all of them animals, but all animals aren't the same. It's about the same thing among humankind. We call all of them humankinds, but all humankinds aren't the same. One group of people is from the seed of the Woman, another group is from the seed of Lucifer and the Gaint, and the last group is born according to the flesh. But we call all of them men and women.

Yahusha made it clear in the book of (**Matthew 13:30**), the tares were the seed of Lucifer and the Giant or those who were born according to the flesh. Watch out the last part of the same verse that says, "But gather the Wheat into my barn." The "wheat" Yahusha spoke about was the seed of the woman in the book of (**Genesis 3:15**). Look at verse 38 in the same book of Matthew chapter 13. The last part says, "But the tares are children of the wicked one." Again, Yahusha spoke about the seed of the serpent in (**Genesis 3:15**)

Look at the first part of verse 38 again. It says, "The field is the whole world." Both seeds live into the same world. They marry together and have children. What will happen again in the last day? The blood will need to be clean again, to dry-clean the blood of the children of the woman before they enter to the kingdom, because the children they had with the children of the Serpent. If the Most High wants them to enter the kingdom, he will purify them before they enter. In total, the whole children of the woman who were among the children of Lucifer, the serpent, will be purified before they get back to the Promised Land (Ezek. 20:33–38), but among the children of the woman, something big will happen also. The rebels and the transgressors the Most High will take them out in the land they sojourn, but they will not enter to the Promised Land (38). They will die in the wilderness of the heathen (35). Those prophecies weren't fulfilled yet.

Most people who read the Book of the Covenant, what people call today the Bible, didn't understand the secret of this book. The Most High didn't reveal the secret to them. Religious organizations kept reading about Cain and Abel, but they never understood why the Most High rejected Cain and chose Abel. Both were born after the sin of their parents. It means both were sinners. Why did the Most High still choose him while he was born after the sin? Both were brothers, both came out from the same womb, both had the same mother, but "both didn't have the same father." Both didn't carry the same bloodline or the same image, because the lineage came from the father, not the mother. Remember what the Most High said before into the book of **(Genesis1:27)**. He created Adam after his own image with the divine bloodline. Adam carried out the Most High's lineage, not his mother, because the mystery mother in the book of **(Genesis 3:15)** is the mother of Adam and Eve also. The mother in the book of **(Revelations 12:1)** is the same mother in the book of **(Genesis 3:15)**. Remember, before something happened into the physical world, it already happened in the invisible world. The two worlds worked together. The mother in the book of **(Genesis 3:15)** wasn't Eve. Eve was in verse 16 the same chapter. The two women weren't the same. So Adam was born or created with the divine blood with the image of his father; therefore, all of Adam's children are supposed to carry out the divine blood and the divine image, but Lucifer transformed himself into the serpent and engineered his sperm into the womb of Eve. He made the eyes of the woman see an animal, but inside the animal was him. He made Eve carry out two different bloodlines.

Now let's talk about the mystery mother on the book of **(Genesis3:15)**. Who was that mystery mother? She was also the mother of the whole creation. Religious organizations read that verse, but they never explained the mystery behind that. Why? Because the founders of all religious organizations in the world are the seeds of Lucifer, the Serpent. The Most High didn't reveal them nothing. They just preached and lied. Read what the Most High said about them in the book of **(Psalm 147:19–20)**. He revealed everything to the seed of the Woman, but didn't reveal anything to the seed of Lucifer, the Serpent. The Most High gave me understanding and wisdom to know the secret. This Woman is the feminine part of the divine family, and the father is the masculine part. Yahusha is the posterity of that Woman who was assassinated by the Roman, the seed of Lucifer, but it's very difficult for the human spirit to describe how the divine family operated in the invisible world. It's too mysterious for us. He created his posterity to live per family, because he had his own family also. That's the way the righteous walk. He did not create you to live one way, then he lived another way. That's not righteous, but this process was only for the seed of the Woman. The heathen, the seed of Lucifer, could live the way they chose too.

Now let's see how the invisible world and the physical world worked together on these two verses, **(Genesis 2:7)** and **(Genesis 1:27)**. Look up the word "created" in verse 27 and the word "formed" in verse 7. Our problem in the physical world is the way we examine things. When we see somebody, the only thing that comes to our minds is **(Genesis 2:7)**, but **(Genesis1:27)** never does. Why? Because we are sleeping deeply, it's hard for us to recognize the importance of the two worlds in the Book of Covenant. Men and women are Spirits (Gen. 1:27) your physical eyes couldn't see. What your physical eyes could see (Gen. 2:7) were the garments. The invisible world was responsible for the real person created and the physical world was responsible for the garments of the real person created into the invisible world. The angels are included, because they were men also. When men and women spoke, the real person inside the garments spoke. The garments itself couldn't talk. If there was no spirit inside it, when someone died, the spirit goes back into the invisible world, because he or she doesn't have a garment to live in the physical world. When a spirit leaves the invisible world to come to the physical world, he must get a physical garment. When he is ready to get back to the invisible world, he loses the garment, because he couldn't live in the invisible world with the physical garment. Remember the Most High created man in his own image, but which one of them? The garment in **(Genesis 2:7)** or Adam created in **(Genesis 1:27)**? The creator is the father of all spirits. Read that for yourself in the book of **(Job 1:6)**. Some lived without physical garments like the angels, some lived with physical garments like the human beings, but when the Most High sent an angel into the physical world to fullfill a mission, he must get a garment. Read that for yourself in to the book of **(Genesis 18:2)** and **(Genesis 19:1)**. Verse 2 in Genesis 18 says three men and verse 1 in Genesis 19 says two angels. These two verses are the same, because the angels are also men. I use the word "garments" to explain the mystery, but it does not mean what we use today to cover ourself. It means our physical garments.

9

Vessel of Honor and Vessel of Dishonor

Let's say you cleaned up your field. You sowed a good seed on it. Let's say, for example, after six or eight weeks, you see all kinds the wild herbs and tares among the good seed you sowed. What will come to your mind? To take all of them out among your good seed, because you didn't sow them. This example explained the whole Book of Covenant from Genesis to Revelation. What people didn't understand in that mystery, the whole earth was created for the posterity of the Woman. Now let's look upon the posterity of the Woman into the book of **(Genesis 5:1–32)**. This chapter mentions each people in each family who carry the image, the likeness, and also carry the royal blood of the Most High. Did all the people in this chapter carry the image, the likeness, and also carry the royal blood of the Most High? The answer is no. This chapter gives the name and the age of each person who carry the image, the likeness, and also carry the royal blood of the Most High.

Let's begin with the name of all the people in **(Genesis 5:1–32)** who carry the image, the likeness, and also carry the royal blood of the Most High not because they weren't sinners, but at least their bloods weren't corrupted with the blood of Lucifer, the ancient

Serpent, because from the root of these people, a pure nation will be born one day. The Most High preserved them from the corrupted blood of the Serpent. The reason why? Abel wasn't mentioned in this chapter. He lost his garment without living a posterity, but in **(Genesis 4:25)**, into the last part of the verse, watched what his father said: "Elohim hath appointed me another seed instead of Abel whom Cain slew." Why did his father say that? Because Abel was supposed to be in the place of Seth. In **(Genesis 5:4)**, you could say Abel was supposed to be the father of Enos. In that case, the invisible body of Abel used another garment called Seth; therefore, Seth typify Abel. Remember the physical world carry the physical garment, but the invisible world carry the real body. One real invisible body could use many different garments in the physical world. An example for us who are living in the physical world, we have many different clothes. Sometimes we change clothes and put on another one, but in the end, we still remain the same person. It is the same for the invisible body in the invisible world.

Now let's come back with the names of all the individuals in **(Genesis 5:1–32)**, but remember all the "dishonored vessels" came out from the "honored vessel." It was a big mystery. You could ask yourself a question. How did that happen? Remember what I said before: what happened in the physical world, already happened in the invisible world. Two groups of people totally different came out from the same root.

In verse 3, Adam begot Seth at 130 years, but in verse 4, Adam begot other sons and daughters. The mystery was there, religious organizations in the world who read the Book of Covenant didn't realize why the name of the other children weren't mentioned in that verse. Because they were born in the flesh. "Dishonored vessel," it was the same. When your cornfield was ready to harvest, you take out the good one and leave the bad one, but all the corns came out from the same root. Only the Most High knew how that happened. All the other good seeds in this chapter begot other sons and daughters, but only the good ones in each family were mentioned.

Number of Years of the Seeds of the Woman in the Physical World

Verse (5) (Adam – 930), verse (8) (Seth – 912), verse (11) (Enos – 950), Verse (14) (Cainan – 910), Verse (17) (Mahalaleel – 895), Verse (20) (Jared – 962), Verse (23) (Enoch – 365), Verse (27) (Methuselah – 969), Verse (30) (Lamech – 595), Genesis 9:29 (Noah – 950)

Why did Ham and Japheth receive the divine blessing from the Most High to be among the good seeds even though they were from the "dishonored vessel"? Let me tell you the reason. The Most High knew in advance he will destroy all flesh with the flood, so he preserved them to carry out the lineage of the "dishonored vessel" because he needs them among the good seeds to accomplish his providence at the end time. Ham and Japheth were born according to the flesh. The Book of Covenant didn't give their age. Now let's continue into Genesis 11:10–32.

Verse (11) (Shem – 500), Verse (13) (Arphaxad – 403), Verse (15) (Salah – 403), Verse (17) (Eber – 430), Verse (19) (Peleg – 209), Verse (21) (Rehu – 207), Verse (23) (Serug – 203), Verse (25) (Nahor – 119),

Verse (27) (Terah – 205), Genesis 25:7 (Abraham – 17), Genesis 35:28 (Isaac – 180), Genesis 47:28 (Jacob 147)

Why did the Book of Covenant give the names and ages of all the people who carried the image, the likeness, and the royal blood, in a total of twenty-two generations from Adam to Jacob? It's because these people were very important to the Most High. Why did the Book of Covenant never mention the names and ages of all the others who lived at the same time with these people? It's because all of them were "dishonored vessels." Why did Terah move from Ur to Canaan with Abraham? It's because Abraham had an important role to play. He could not play that role where he was, or any other place in the world. He had to move to the center of the world. Read for yourself Ephesians 1:4, to see what Apostle Paul said concerning the seed of the Woman. If Paul was here with us now to read my book, he will know the mystery I'm talk about. Watch the pronoun "we" in that verse. It means only the seed of the Woman, not everybody in the world. This is the mystery many people who read the Book of Covenant didn't understood. Everything is already set up in the invisible world. What is left is only to realize it in the physical world.

From Adam to Jacob, 11,619 years was the time to select the seed of the Woman for the kingdom by age. They already chose before the foundation of the world. They had to be born into the physical world among the twenty-two generations. Women were also chosen, but in the divine mystery, women didn't count. These twenty-two generations stand for the twenty-two letters of the original Hebrew alphabet.

Remember all things were created by Yahusha, the first word of the father and the first word became son of the father. This word is the Hebrew root of all the other words. The Most High moved Abraham from Ur to Canaan. At the time this place wasn't called Jerusalem because two sacrifices had to be made by Abraham before this place had to be called the physical mother named Jerusalem. The first sacrifice (Gen.15:7–10) was to divide the good seed and the bad seed, but in verse 10, Abraham didn't divide the birds, which means the good seed and the bad seed will still live together. Now the second sacrifice (Gen. 22:7–10), Abraham was victorious, because this sacrifice was to establish the foundation of faith, but in **(Genesis 15:13–14)**, read what the Most High said to Abraham. Because the turtledove and the young pigeon weren't divided, if Abraham also divided them, it means the seed of the Woman and the seed of the Serpent will be completely divided forever. There will be no seed of the Serpent among the seed of the Woman, but by not dividing them, the seed of the Serpent is still among the seed of the Woman until now. In the invisible world, the Most High already decided to send his son into the physical world to save the seed of the Woman from the seed of the Serpent, but before he sent his own son, he must find among the seed of the Woman in the physical world one man who had enough faith to sacrifice his own son; therefore, the one he found among the seed of the Woman was Abraham.

From the time of Adam to Jacob, only twenty-two people carried the image, the likeness, and the royal blood of the Most High, even though some of them worshipped false deity. For example, according to **(Jasher 9:8)**, Terah, the father of Abraham, had twelve gods and worshipped one every month. The same thing happened in our time today. Many of the seeds of the Woman who are among the heathen today worship the false deity. Read that for yourself in **(Revelations 12:9)**. Look at what the old Serpent did to deceive the whole seeds of the Woman who were among his people. He even deceived his own people. He doesn't care since he kept the seed of the Woman in ignorance. The big problem of the old Serpent is he does not want the seeds of the Woman who were among his people to know who they are; hence, he kept them in ignorance. He will rule the whole earth for a long time with his people. This is the old Serpent's destination.

In (Genesis15:18–21), Elohim promised Abraham the land of ten different people. All those lands were called the land of Canaan. Africa wasn't the original name of those areas. Among those areas, Jebusites was the center of the world. Abraham gave tithes to Melchizedek, king of Salem. It was the same area that King David chose to be the capital of the country of Israel at a later time, "Yerushalayim" (1 Chron. 11:4–5). Therefore the word "Jerusalem" today came out from the words "Yerushalayim," "Jebus," and "Salem.

Why did Elohim choose this area? It was the center of the world (Zech.12:2, Ezek. 5:5, and Ezek. 38:12). This area will become the breastfeeding for the descendants of Abraham from Isaac to Jacob, but not all the other sons, or everybody in the world, like the Christian churches preach today.

The birth of Abraham was very famous. One star came out from the east and swallowed up four stars, in the four corners in the world. What does this phenomenon symbolized? At that time Nimrod was the Chaldeen king. Because of this mysterious event, Nimrod asked Terah to bring Abraham to him to destroy him, but Terah didn't bring Abraham to him. He brought him another child he had with one of his concubines. The Most High was with Terah to protect Abraham from the assassin. This mysterious event means the descendants of Abraham from Isaac to Jacob will inherit the four corners in the world. Read that for yourself in (Jasher 5:1–36). Read also, in the (Revelations 21:12–13), the twelve sons of Jacob, who were the descendants of Abraham, who occupied the twelve three dimensional doors in the creation. The apostles who were the descendants of Abraham also occupied the twelve three dimensional foundations in the world (therefore Revelations 21:12–14 and Jasher 5:1–36, precept upon precept).

Abraham did everything the Most High told him to do, but by not completely dividing the turtledove and the young dove, the same thing that happened in the time of Adam between Cain and Abel will happene again in the time Isaac between Esau and Jacob, because the seed of the Woman wasn't completely divided from the seed of the Serpent, Lucifer. If Abraham divided all the animals, the good and evil were completely separared, why didn't Abraham divide them? Because Abraham's job stopped there. Now the posterity of Abraham from the Woman in **(Genesis 3:15)** will finish the job. The good and evil must remain together until the end time. Who will finish the job completely? Read for yourself in **(Matthew 25:31–34)**. In verse 33, look what will happen. The posterity of Abraham will finish the job in **(Genesis 15:9)**. The sheep symbolizes the seed of the Woman in **(Genesis 3:15)**. The kingdom was prepared for them before the foundation of the physical world. The posterity of Abraham from the Woman, who will finish the job at the end of time, was Yahusha. Now look what the Most High told Abraham regarding his descendants in **(Genesis 15:13)** because the good and evil still remain together. The seeds of the Woman will be in slavery in the hands of the seeds of the Serpent, and the other nations who were born according to the flesh compromised with the seeds of the Serpent to punish the seeds of the Woman until the end of time. At the end of time, the table will turn for the seeds of the Woman. Read that for yourself in **(Luke 21:24)**. This verse means the seeds of the Woman will serve all nations into captivity before the end of time.

Let me tell you how the divine principle works. If you want to be at the head in the end, you have to serve others first. The Messiah didn't come to be served, but to serve others (Matt. 20:28). In the end the seeds of the Woman will possess the rest of the seeds of the Serpent, and the rest of all other nations who were born according to the flesh, some of them will be servants and handmaids, some of them will be in captivities forever (Isa. 14:2).

Remember I said the good and evil still remained together into the root of Abraham, because the animals were not completely divided. Abraham had eight sons but only Isaac among them was born according to the image, the likeness, and the royal blood (Gen. 21:1–7). The rest of the seven sons were born according to the flesh. One good thing Abraham was victorious in the sacrifice of Isacc. The foundation of faith was established for the Messiah to come. Remember all works of the Most High is accompanied with symbol and full with wisdom. To understand his past or his future, he has to call you and give you wisdom of understanding. Other than that, you will pretend you understand his work, but finally you understood nothing. He didn't open your eyes. Not because your physical eyes were opened. That's enough for you to understand his work. Your physical eyes couldn't see nothing in the invisible world. He had to give you the eyes of the invisible world to understand his work. Because what you see in the physical world is a copy of what happened in the invisible world. Let me give an example. Read for yourself the experience of Steven in the book of **(Acts 7:55)**. In this case people who were very close with him didn't see what he saw in that vision, because Steven had double eyes. He could see things other people couldn't see. Another example in the book of 2 **(Kings 6:15–17)**, in verse (15) the servant spoke to Elisha about the Syrian army. In verse (16), Elisha told him the army of the Most High is already with us, but he couldn't see what Elisha see (16) because his invisible eyes weren't opened. In verse (17) Elisha prayed for the Most High to open his eyes. Those examples showed us that not because someone had ability to read the book of the covenant, they understood it.

Lucifer still had an important role to play, into the roots of Abraham, similar to the one he had played in the time of Adam between Cain and Abel. Now Abraham accomplished everything the Most High want him to accomplish. Lucifer was waiting for his time to invade after Sarah's death and Abraham was very old. Read what he said to his servant in **(Genesis 24:2–3)**: to put his hand upon his thigh. Why did he ask him to vow before the Most High not to take a wife for his son Issac among the Canaanites people? It seems like there was something Abraham knew. Who wasn't in the Book of Covenant? A mystery we never had preached by religious organizations today. In the book of **(Genesis 9:22)**, why did Ham commit sin, and in verse 25, why did Noah curse Canaan? What was the mystery behind that? Noah was supposed to cursed Ham, not Canaan. In chapter 10 verse 6, why didn't Noah curse Mizraim. To understand this mystery, you have to ask yourself all these questions. The Book of Covenant explained clearly the mystery of discovering the nakedness of your father, but without precept upon precept, you will never understand this mystery. The mystery of discovering your father's nakedness means have sex with your father's wife.

After the flood, Lucifer the Serpent influenced Ham to have sex with one of his father's wives. Remember sin was transmitted by blood, generation to generation. In this case, Canaan was the son of Lucifer per Ham and also carried the Serpent's blood. Let me show you clearly in the Book of Covenant the language of discovering the nakedness of your father. **(Leviticus18:8)**, precept upon precept, makes it clear to understand verse 22 in the book of Genesis chapter 9. In this case, Ham did not really discover the nakedness of his father, but one of his father's wives; therefore, Noah cursed Canaan, the son Ham had with one of his wives.

To better understand the language of what happened between Ham and his father Noah in **(Genesis 9:21–25)**, you have to read Leviticus chapter 18. Now you will realize what discovery of your father's nakedness means. Remember I said before Abraham knew something about the Canaanites people that wasn't written in the Book of Covenant. That's why he made his servant swear not to take a wife for Isaac among the Canaanites people. He knew for sure the Canaanites people carried the Serpent's blood. He didn't want the royal blood to be mixed with the Canaanites' blood. Abraham did not care if the six other sons he had with Keturah took their wives among the Canaanites, even Ishmael, but for Isaac, it's different. He told his servant to go back to his kindred and take a wife for Isaac (Gen. 24:6). He told his servant, Isaac must remain where he was and wasn't allowed to go with the servant. Why? Abraham knew Isaac was different from the seven other sons. He had to remain closed to his primordial mother to breastfeed, where the center of the world was. This invisible mother wasn't the mother of the other seven sons, because they were born according to the flesh. Abraham knew Isaac's wife must come from Shem descendants, who wasn't affected by the Serpent's blood.

The servant went to Mesopotamia, in the city of Nahor, Abraham's grandfather, and found Rebekah for Isaac (Gen. 24:67).

Other names for the Jebusites area, or Jerusalem, was Tzion, Syyon, Syon, and Sion. Looked what David said about that area in the book of **(Psalm 87:2–3)**. This area was also the residence of the Most High (Heb. 12:22). It's also the umbilical cord of the world. If you look at yourself, you will see the whole world in you, because your umbilical cord was placed to the center of your body; it means the Most High created man the same way he created the world. It was the residence of the invisible mother of the good seeds. Everywhere they went in the world like slave because of sin. One day they had to come back there for breastfeeding. That's why Rebekah left Mesopotamia to join Isaac there, because Rebekah was also the daughter of Shem. Religious organizations in the world don't understand this mystery, because they don't worship the "Elohim" of Abraham, of Isaac, and of Jacob. They worship the Egyptian god-head-dog deity, and they associate our forefathers' name with that deity. Our forefathers didn't worship god. They worshipped the creator whose name was designed with the twenty-two original Hebrew letters, not god.

In **(Genesis 5:1–32)** and **(Genesis 11:10–32)**, all these people were born with the Hebrew language on them. One example in the book of Genesis told us that Adam gave names to all animals in Hebrew (Gen.2:19–20). Where did he go to school to lean all these names? Nowhere.

Now looked what the Most High told Abraham in **(Genesis 15:15)**: "After death you will go to your father in peace." Which group of people did the Most High say Abraham will meet after death? The group of nineteen generations, from Adam to Terah. All these people Spirits who carried the image, the likeness, and the royal blood of the Most High were in the same place after death. We have another example, in the book of **(Deuteronomy 32:50)**. The Most High told Moses the same thing, Aaron also, in **(Numbers 20:24 and 28)**. In this case, Moses, Aaron, and all the twelve tribes were in the same place with the twenty-two generations after death. Remember all these people carried the image, the likeness, and the royal blood of the Most High. They weren't in the same place with the heathen after death.

But Dan was not among them. Dan was among the heathen after death. Look what Jacob told Joseph when he arrived in Egypt (Gen. 48:5–6). Jacob knew, at the last, he will need Manasseh to replace Dan among the twelve tribes (Rev. 7:5–8) because Dan didn't carry the image, the likeness, and the royal blood. Read what Jacob said about Dan in **(Genesis 49:16–17)**. Jacob identified Dan with the same Serpent (Gen.3:15) and the same viper as Yahusha identified the Edomite in **(Matthew 12:34)**. In this case, Dan did carry the image and the Serpent blood. Jacob knew, at the last also, he will need Ephraim to be the head or the chief of the ten tribes. That's why he told Joseph he would adopt these two boys (Ezek. 37:19) because Jacob knew Dan would not remain among the tribes. He would be a snare for them (Jer. 8:16–17). In verse 17, the "you" means the other eleven tribes including Manasseh, but because they disobeyed the Most High, "cockatrices and serpents among you, will bite you," meaning the descendants of Dan would be among them to prosecute them as Jacob, the father of Dan, said in **(Genesis 49:17)**, precept upon precept **(Jeremiah 8:17)** and **(Genesis 49:17)**. Dan was born according to the flesh, and he was among the heathen as judged until the endtime (Gen. 49:16).

Remember I said Lucifer the Serpent is waiting for his time again. Rebekah, the wife of Isaac, was barren. Isaac prayed to the Most High and the Most High granted his prayers. Rebekah conceived (Gen. 25:21–22). Rebekah wasn't comfortable during the time of the pregnancy, and she prayed to the Most High and the Most High answered her. In verse 23, the Most High said to her two babies were in her womb, and two nations were in your womb. Why did the Most High say that? Because the Most High knew, in the future, the personal names of these two boys, Esau and **(Jacob (25–26))**, will change for two biblical names, Edom and Israel. Edom was the biblical and nation name for the descendants of Esau (30). Israel was the biblical and nation name for the descendants of Jacob (Gen. 32:28). People thought Jacob stole the birthright of Esau, without knowing the mystery behind that, but they never asked themselves this question: who was Esau? Remember the evil was still in the root of Abraham, because the turtledove and the young dove were not divided (Gen.15:10). Now let me repeat: the same thing that happened in the time of Adam between Cain and Abel, the same thing happened again in the time Isaac between Esau and Jacob. In this case, Jacob didn't steal the birthright of Esau. The blessing must change course. The Most High knew beforehand what will happen. Lucifer the Serpent will have a son again in the place of the descendants of Cain, his son who was destroyed in the flood. Everything you read in **(Genesis 25:19–34)** and **(Genesis 27:1–46)** came from the Most High. This was the way he wanted that to happen, because he knew Esau better than Esau knew himself. He won't let Esau have the blessing. Isaac had nothing to do other than accomplish the wisdom of the Most High between Esau and Jacob, because his mighty hand controlled Isaac's family.

Why did Abraham teach the way of the Most High to Jacob, but not to Esau? Read that in **(Jasher 16:28)**. He already knew Jacob was the seed of the Woman. Another example, why did Jacob go to the house of Shem? Again to learn the way of the Most High. Read that again in **(Jasher 18:18)**. Jacob was the one who will continue the seed of the Woman until the end of time, not Esau. These three servants of the Most High—Abraham, Isaac, and Jacob—were the root someone came from, in their time. Today Christians don't believed in it. They believed in the blood of Jesus Christ, meaning Julius Ceasar, the first dictator of the Roman Empire. The apostle Paul understood very well what his forefathers believed, when he wrote under divine inspiration.

In **(Romans 11:16)**, he spoke in that verse about two important elements, first "fruit" and "root." These two words were a reference to his forefathers. Paul knew what our forefathers Abraham, Isaac, and Jacob did to preserve the root because he knew his forefathers were very careful to keep the root pure. Remember what the Most High said in the beginning. He created man to his own image, according to his likeness. Adam was created like that. Now people don't understand what sin means. It means the blood is corrupt; it needs to be washed out.

There are two verses in the Book of Covenant that religious organizations don't pay attention to: **(Genesis 1:27)** and **(Genesis**

3:15). Those two verses explain the whole Book of Covenant if you understand the mysteries behind them, but only some of the seeds of the Woman, not all of them, will receive wisdom from the Most High. Watch the two words "wicked" and "wise" in (Daniel 12:10). Who will be wise to understand the mysteries in that book? Only some of the seeds of the Woman, because this book is for them. Who will never understand this book? The seeds of the Serpent Lucifer, or those who were born according to the flesh and the rest of the Giants who are still among us. Now one nation was born from the root of the twenty-two generations, from Adam to Jacob, whose names and ages were given by the Book of Covenant.

The Seed of the Woman Became the Nation of Israel

"Israel" was the biblical name and nation name for Jacob. Was mystery word there only at the time Jacob was qualified to receive symbolic name? No. This mystery word was there since the creati Adam was supposed to receive this symbolic name, but because Ad: and his wife failed, the Most High cleared the way for 11,619 yea until someone among the seeds of the Woman was qualified to recei this symbolic name. All the preparations the Most High made was reestablished the seeds of the Woman as they were in the invisible worl but because of the long time it took, the seeds of Lucifer the Serpe was still among them to prosecute them.

Before Jacob received that name, he must meet with Yahush: Where did he meet with him? People think the "stone" Jacob chos for his pillow while he left Canaan to Mesopotamia was a simple ston (Gen. 28:11). This was the same rock Moses used to give water to th seeds of the Woman (Num. 20:8 and 11). Yahusha spoke also about th same stone in **(Matthew 21:41 and 44)**. The prophet Daniel saw the same stone (Dan. 2:34). All these mysteries about the stone combined to one Yahusha. In that case, the mystery stone Jacob used that night as pillow was Yahusha. He stayed all the night with Jacob. Read verses

12–13 of the same chapter of Genesis (28). What happened that night was the proof Yahusha was there with Jacob.

Now let's see at the end of time who will inherit the whole earth, the kingdom, and the eternal life" (Gen.13:14–16). Watch what the Most High told Abraham after Lot was separated from him. Why did the Most High wait for Lot to go? Because Lot came from Shem, and also, Lot wasn't the seed of Lucifer the Serpent. Lot wasn't part of this heritage, because Lot was born according to the flesh. He was a good man who received the messengers of the Most High with great respect (Gen. 19:1–11), but that still did not qualify him to be among the seeds of the Woman. In verse 14 in Genesis chapter 13, the Most High told Abraham to look northward to southward to eastward and westward. Now read verse 15 of the same chapter. Look for the word "seed." It means someone who came out from your bowels. Now you may think that all the sons of Abraham came out from his bowels, all of them are the same. No, the Most High spoke to Abraham about Isaac, Sarah's son, not Ishmael or the others six sons he had with Keturah. When the Most High told Abraham to look at the four dimensions of the world, it didn't mean only where the eyes of Abraham could see, but also where his eyes couldn't see. Let me give you an example: at the time where Abraham stood, his eyes couldn't see Europe and America, but those areas were also included. Read Jasher chapter 8 to see what happened on the night Abraham was born, specifically verses 2–3. Don't under estimate the book of Jasher because the Book of Covenant mentioned it in **(Joshua 10:13)** and again in 2 **(Samuel 1:18)**. Now the seed of the Most High from Abraham was Isaac, not Ishmael or the others six sons of Keturah. The seed of the Most High from Isaac was Jacob, not Esau, and the seed of the Most High from Jacob were the eleven tribes including the Manasses equal to the twelve tribes, not including Dan.

The mysteries between Abraham to Jacob already happened in the invisible world. In that situation, Abraham typified the Most High (Gen. 22:7–8), Isaac typified Adam (Gen. 25:25–26), Rebekah typified Eve (Gen. 25:23), Esau typified Cain (Gen. 26:41), Jacob typified Abel (Gen. 29: 22), Sarah typified the Woman in **(Genesis 3:15)**. All these things already happened in the invisible world before they manifested in the physical world. Let me give you an example how generation continue to be reborn into the same generation.

Malachi announced under the divine inspiration that Elijah the prophet must come before Yahusha came. Elisabeth, the wife of Zacharias, conceived. Read that in **(Luke 1:24–25)**. In the same chapter, in verses 57–66, Elisabeth gave birth to his son. His name was John. But remember the Most High took Elijah. Elisha saw Elijah went up by a whirlwind into heaven. Read that for yourself in verse 2 **(Kings 2:1–14)**. Elijah didn't go to the invisible world with both garments, his physical body or his own clothes verse 12. Malachi prophesied Elijah must come again before Yahusha came to prepare the way before him. The question was, how will he come again? He lost the physical body he used to live in before. Now he will leave the invisible world to come back to the physical world. He will need a new garment, because he will not use the previous one. The second garment will not be called the same name with the previous one. This principle show us how the two worlds worked together to accomplish the Most High's providence. When Malachi announced Elijah must come, he didn't talk about Elijah's physical body, but the Spirit. Now when the time came for the Spirit to come again, the Most High chose Zacharias and Elisabeth to be the father and the mother of the garment named John for the Spirit to enter. Even the disciples of Yahusha didn't know John was Elijah based on the question they asked Yahusha. Read that for yourself in **(Matthew 17:10)**. In verse 12, Yahusha revealed this mystery to them. In verse

13, the disciples knew John was Elijah who Malachi announced in his book (Mal. 4:5). Also in **(Matthew 11:13–15)**, Yahusha made it clear the Spirit who was inside Elijah the garment was now inside John the new garment. Each garment had a different name (precept upon precept Mark1:6 and 2 Kings 1:8.) Yahusha made it clear again, in **(John 6:63)**, the flesh is nothing. It is a garment for the Spirit. (What was important for the Most High? Only the Spirit and life only).

Today it's very difficult for people who read the Book of Covenant to understand what I explain in this book, because they aren't connected with the invisible world. This example shows us how generation of Spirit continues to be reborn into the same generation to continue the providence of the Most High until the end of time. Now the seed of the Woman was almost separated from the seed of Lucifer the Serpent, but two things must happen again, into the root of Abraham.

Why was Rebekah barren? There was a reason for that. Anything you read about this group of people, there was a mystery behind that. She must wait until the time the Most High designed to put the garment of the two nations inside her womb—one garment for the Spirit who was inside the garment Cain, who will be called Esau, the new garment; the other garment for the Spirit who was inside the garment Abel will be called Jacob, the new garment. Remember the Spirit inside Cain killed the garment of the Spirit inside Abel. What the Spirit of Cain did to the Spirit of Abel didn't stop the Most High's providence. When Isaac prayed to the Most High for his wife (Gen. 25:21), it means the time had come for the Most High to remove the bareness (years years), half Isaac's age when he lived with Rebekah (40 + 20 = 60). The age of Isaac when the two boys were born, in verse 22, was sixty. The two boys wrestled between them. In verse 26, Jacob's hand held the heel of Esau. People read the Book of Covenant, but don't understand the mystery behind that. What does the heel mean to your whole body? It means the end.

30

The head is the starting part of your body until the heel. It means the whole body of Esau symbolized the first world, starting upon the head until the heel. Now the hand held the heel, what you do the first time you see something is to touch that with your hand. It means beginning. The hand of Jacob will control the second world forever, because there is no end for the hand and after the heel, there is nothing. This signifies "the descendants of Esau will be the ruler of the first world under the governance of Lucifer until the end or the heel, Now the descendants of Jacob will be the ruler of the second world, under the governance of the Most High forever "hand." Now Jacob had the vision of ladder when he was on his way to Mesopotamia (Gen. 28:12). In verse 17, Jacob called that place the universal door of the universe. He must have had this mysterious vision before the twelve tribes came out from his bowels. Now he had the second vision when he was on his way back from Mesopotamia to Canaan (Gen. 32:24). Now in verse 28, the Most High spoke to him about his fight with Elohim and his fight with Esau and Laban, his father-in-law. Jacob must pass those tests to receive the nation name "Israel" in (Gen. 32:28). The Most High accomplished what he told Rebekah in **(Genesis 25:23)**: "two nations are in your bowels. "I In **(Genesis 35:9)**, the Most High appeared to Jacob again and affirmed him. "Your name will change from Jacob to Israel." Now Jacob was the twenty-second person from the generation for whom the Book of Covenant gave the names and ages of each of them. It took 11,619 years to clean the root of this generation before someone from the seed of the Woman was qualified to give birth to twelve sons minus Dan, or eleven sons who carried the image, the likeness, and the royal blood of the divine family.

Now Jacob, the last seed of the Woman from the twenty-two generations, was the father of the eleven tribes plus Manasseh, who he adopted from Joseph, or twelve tribes who fully carried the image, the likeness, and the royal blood of the divine family. Now the Most High was ready to build a divine nation without any trace of Lucifer's blood among them. But Dan was still among them. He was not replaced yet, so one major thing must happen again. Why did Joseph have these two visions (Gen. 37:7–10)? Joseph had a double honors among the other tribes, because in the future, Manasseh will replace Dan and Ephraim will be the head of the ten northern tribes in Samaria. In this case, the eleven brothers hate him. In verse 18, they conspired against him to kill him. In verse 22, they threw him into the pit. In verse 28, they sold him to the Ishmaelites. The Ishmaelites brought him into Egypt. In verse 31, they killed a kid and dipped Joseph's coat into the blood. In verse 33, Jacob recognized his son's coat, saying an evil beast devoured him. In verse 36, when he arrived in Egypt, the Midianites sold him unto Potiphar. Now two things happened: Dan was still among them and their brothers hated him. For these two visions, so evil was spilled among them, for all evil things they did to Joseph, the Most High couldn't use them now to build the divine nation. They must pay all the bad things they did to Joseph before the Most High used them to built the divine nation.

Now they will pay "teeth for teeth," all the evil things they did to Joseph. The Most High hit Canaan with strong famine (Gen. 42:2). Jacob said unto his sons, "Go to Egypt to buy corn." Now read verses 6–7 to see what happened. Compare **(Genesis 37:7)** with **(Genesis 42:6)**. They bowed down before him the same way Joseph saw in that vision. Read Genesis chapter 42 to chapter 44. You will see on those chapters, Joseph's brothers paid only half of the evil they did to him. The Most High gave Joseph wisdom to chastise them for all they did to him in the land of Canaan. The rest of the evil they did their descendants will pay in the land of Egypt because Joseph was mistreated in the land of Canaan and Egypt. After they paid half of the evil they did to Joseph, look what the Most High told Jacob (Gen. 46:3) while he was on his way to Egypt. "Now the nation of the seed of the Woman will be formed in Egypt (Gen. 3:15)."

Joseph's brothers threw him unto the pit after that they sat down together to eat. When they saw the Ishmaelites, they took him out from the pit and sold him to them. They took his clothes, they let him go hungry with the Ishmaelites. When he arrived in Egypt, the Ishmalites sold him to Potiphar as a slave. After thirteen years, the brothers of Joseph followed the same way, also hungry, to go to Egypt, to bow down before Joseph for foods. This was the wisdom of the Most High. Now the seeds of the Woman became a nation in the land of Egypt and lived in peace and multiplied among the Egyptians for around 122 years. But **(Exodus 1:8–10)** spoke about a new Pharaoh who did not know Joseph, because Joseph died before he rose as a king (Gen. 50:25–26). Did the new Pharaoh do that deliberately? The answer is no. The Most High changed the heart of the new Pharaoh against the descendants of the ten brethren of Joseph, because they had to pay the rest of the evil their fathers did to Joseph while they lived in Canaan in peace and Joseph in slavery in the house of Potipha. The Most High took Joseph first before he made them pay the rest of their evil. People who read the Book of Covenant thought the seeds of the Woman that suffered slavery in Egypt was the one the Most High told Abraham in **(Genesis 15:13)**, that four hundred years were before the seeds of the Woman received the Ten Commamdements from the Most High, but there were four hundred years again. In **(Leviticus 26:18, 21, 24, 28)**, each of this verse mentioned (100), two times seven equal (49) + 1=50 + 50=100 years. One time (100) years for each of this verse equals (400) years also. There was a little problem here. **(Exodus 12:40)** said (430) years. **(Acts 7:6 said)** (400) years. **(Genesis 15:13)** said (400) years also. The Book of Covenant said, in 2 **(Corinthians 13:1)** and **(Deuteronomy 17:6)**, says the same thing: a matter must be resolved with the mouth of two or three witnesses, but not the mouth of one witness (Deut. 19:15). These two verses count for truth. The problem was that, if they expended (400) years in Egypt, but they didn't expect (400) years in slavery, that (400) years must be taken from the time Joseph entered Egypt and the time he died, because they weren't punished yet for rest of the evil their fathers did to Joseph. He expended (13) years of slavery in the house of Potipha, and he ordered his servants to whip Joseph for the account of his lying wife and put him in prison. All that mistreatment were caused by his ten brethren. So that (400) years must be calculated like that, when Joseph entered Egypt, he was (17) years old. He died at (110) years old (110 - 17 =93). Seventeen years in Canaan, ninety-three years in Egypt, now (400 - 93 = 307 years) while (307) years, the Most High multiplied them in Egypt, but before he took them out of Egypt, he let Pharaoh enslave them for (93) years to pay the rest of the evil their fathers did to Joseph, so (307+93=400) years. Read **(Exodus 20:5)** to see how the Most High punished iniquity of the fathers, upon the children, generation to generation. That exactly happened to them.

Now why Jacob, the twenty-second person from the twenty-two generations have twelve tribes (Rev. 7:5–8)? Because the world was divided in twelve parts, one part for each tribe, but the tribe of Joseph had two parts—Joseph one part, Manasseh one part. What the Most High told Abraham, Isaac, and Jacob, in Genesis. The Most High showed John that in the book of Revelation, but the Most High didn't reveal that to the religious leaders of the world, because they weren't his servants. He didn't call them. To understand the heritage already divided among the twelve tribes, you must use the divine principle "precepts." Let me show how it already happened.

The Most High Accomplished His Promises

(Abraham) (Gen. 13:14–16), (Ez. 48:30–35), (Rev. 21:11–13); (Isaac) (Gen. 26:3–4), (Ez. 48:30–35), (Rev. 21:11–13); (Jacob) (Gen. 28:13–14), (Ez. 48:30–35), (Rev. 21:11–13)

Watched the (4) times (3) universal doors equal (12) doors. In verse (13), in the four corners of the world, read the same principle in **(Exodus 28:15–19)**. The (4) times (3) settings of stones equal (12) stones, and now read the foundations of the world, in Revelation 21:14, the twelve apostles of Yahusha. Now read the prophets, in **(Revelation 21: 18–20)**. The prophets were parts of the foundations also. So the whole world was shared among the seed of the Woman. What the Most High told Abraham, Isaac, and Jacob in the book of Genesis, he did it in Revelation. The reason why? It wasn't manifested yet in the physical form. There was a remnant of the seed of the Woman, meaning the descendants of Abraham, Isaac, and Jacob scattered among the heathen. At the end of time, the Most High will bring them back, in their heritage depending on the tribe they came from. Read the remnant of the seed of the Woman in **(Revelation 12:17)**. She was the same Woman in **(Genesis 3:15)**. The Most High didn't share anything with the heathen. All personalities in the book of Revelation chapter

(21) are the seed of the Woman. Why did the Book of Covenant say, in **(Revelation 22:19)**, "Don't take away anything from the deal?" Because the heritage was already shared among the members. Case closed. Don't put anything in, don't take anything out, because the contract was already signed between the two parties. People who read the book don't understand the mystery. All you read from the book of Genesis to Revelation, including the Apocrypha are the covenant between the Most High and the seed of the Woman only. The other nationalities like Japheth, Ham, Ishmael, Esau, Lot, and the rest of four sons of Shem, Elam, Asshur, Lud, Aram (Gen. 10:22) and also the six sons Abraham had with Keturah (Gen. 25:2), the rest of the Giants weren't included in the covenant. All these people were born according to the flesh. They didn't carry the image, the likeness, and the royal blood of the divine family (Gen. 1:27). These people were born to be the slaves, the servants of the seed of the Woman (Lev. 25:44–46).

Now the seed of the Woman became a nation. It needed a shepherd. Religious leaders who read the Book of Covenant but don't understand the work of the Most High among the children of men thought Moses just fled to Midian by himself. The answer is no. The time will come for the Most High to deliver his nation. He took Moses among the seed of the Woman and transported him to Midian to learn to be a shepherd. Even Pharaoh's daughter who gave the name Moses to the boy didn't do it just like that. This name came from the Most High to her mouth (Ex. 2:10). Moses grew up as a prince, not a shepherd. That's why the Most High sent him to Midian to Jethro's house (Ex. 3:1) to learn that skill behind the sheeps, before he sent him back to Egypt, before Pharaoh, to deliver his people from slavery.

When Moses was born, the seed of the Woman already got (13) years in slavery. When Moses fled to Midian at (40) years old, the seed of the Woman had (53) years in slavery. Moses remained for (40) years in Midian and went back to Egypt at (80) years old to deliver them. (80-13=93) years in slavery. (400-93=307) years prosperities. After he delivered them, he remained (40) years with them (80+40=120) years. Now after 12, 019 years (11,619+400=12,019) years, the seed of the Woman become a nation. Now the Most High will give them the law of life. Moses was the mediator between the Most High and the nation of Israel.

Let's look at what Moses must do before he received the law. The principle of (40) days and (40) nights means one morning of (12) hours and one evening of (12) hours equal to one day of (24). (40) times days and nights equal (20) days of (24) hours, (24) multiplied by (20) equal (480) hours, without eating bread and drinking water. The Most High instructed him the statutes, the judgments, and the law to teach the seed of the Woman. It was the process of purification before Moses could touch the tablets of the law. Moses has (3) times (40) days and (40) nights (Jasher 82:9), (40) days and (40) nights (Ex. 24:18), (40) days and (40) nights (Ex. 34:28), (40) days and (40) nights, so (3) times (40) days and (40) nights, (3) multiplied by (20) equal (60) days of (24) hours. Now (3) times (480) hours equal (1440) hours without eating bread or drinking water. Moses stayed half of his age with the Most High (60) days without communicating with any human being. According to the formula (1) day for (1) year (60+60=120) years of the life of Moses.This mystery of (60) days with the Most High signified a total separation between Moses and the world's sinners, meaning Moses became sinless, before the Most High could give him this law. This process showed us the importance of this law (Ex. 20:1–17).

Let's see what the lineage of the seed of the Woman who became the nation of Israel answer to the Most High concerning this covenant in **(Exodus 24:7–8)**. In verse 7, the seed of the Woman said, "All that the Most High hath said will we do and be obedient." In verse 8, Moses sprinkled the blood upon all of them.

The covenant included not to marry to the other nations (Deut. 7:3, Ez. 10:17–18), not to make a treaty with them (Ex. 34:12, Ex. 23:32–33), be obedient to the commamdments without turning right or left (Deut. 28:14, Prov. 4:27), not to worship other deities (Ex. 23:13, Ex. 23:24). In total, the seed of the Woman must be pure in Spirit and body. This was the big difference. The Most High wanted to establish between his heritage, the house of Jacob, and the other nations. The covenant was conditional—if the house of Jacob remained obedient to all commandments, not some of them. The covenant included laws, ordinances, precepts, statutes, and judgments. Now read the blessing the house of Jacob will receive between **(Deut.28:2-14)**. Now read the punishments the house of Jacob will receive between **(Deut.28:16-68)**. Now in **(Leviticus 26:1–3)**, if the house of Jacob remained obedient to all "commandments," not some of them, read the blessing between verses (4–13), but if the house of Jacob despised the covenant (14–15), read the punishments the house of Jacob will receive between the verses 16–46. The covenant was only for the house of Jacob, meaning, the descendants of the twelve tribes of Israel, the seed of the Woman in Genesis 3:15. The Almighty made his covenant only with this group of people who carries his image, his likeness, and the royal blood. The other nations are not included in this covenant, because some of them are the seed of Lucifer the Serpent, some of them are born according to the flesh, some of them are the rest of the Giants. They look like normal human being, but they do not carry the image, the likeness, and the royal blood (Gen. 1:27). Because the mystery is that, the image, the likeness are not something you can see physically. Only the descendants of the twelve tribes who came from the lineage of the twenty-two generations carried those qualities (Gen. 1:27 and Gen. 5:1–2).

If the house of Jacob kept the covenant, without turning right or left, read in (**Deutoronomy 4:5–7**) the way they will be, and also, they will be the head of all nations on the earth (Deut. 28:1), but by despising the covenant, read the way they will be in (**Deutoronomy 28:43**). The last part of the verse is "you will come down very low." An example is the Haitians in Haiti, the lineage of the priesthood. They were supposed to be the priests of the Most High. Instead of that, they became the priests of Lucifer, the ancient Serpent. Why? Because the Haitians blessings were changed in curse. Read this in (**Malachi 2:1–2**). Now read verse 3: the Most High spread the "dung" of the Haitians solemn feasts into the Haitians faces. In verse 9, read the way the Haitians become, in the eyes of all nations now, "an astonishment,a proverb, and a byword." Why did the Haitians receive more punishments than the other tribes? Because the Most High chose the Levites for his firstborn among the others tribes. Read that in the book of (**Numbers 8:5–26**). In this case, the Levites were closer to the Most High. They were responsible also for the service, in the tabernacle of the congregation. Read this in Numbers chapter 18. The word "stranger" in verse 4 means the others tribes. It does not mean the other nations. In verse 23, the Most High said, "There will be no inheritance, for the Levites, among the children of Israel." It will be a statute for ever. In the last part of verse 20, the Most High said to the Levites, "I am your inheritance, among the children of Israel." In that case, the Levites were placed in a high position, meaning after the "Almighty" the other tribes came after the Levites. When you are in a very high position, if you make a mistake, you will fall down very low. The Haitians people, my people, the descendants of the priest, became very low in the eyes of all nations around the world (Mal. 2:9). Now when another nation think about Haiti or the Haitians people, the only things that come to their minds are diseases, contemptibles, bases, dungs, muddles, and muds. Malachi chapter 1 and 2 were only for the priesthood. The Levites despised the covenant of the Most High (Mal.1:6). The Most High made them contemptibles and bases (Mal. 2:9). Precept upon precept, "You despised my covenant. I made you contemptibles and bases. You did it in secret. I did it in public." This prophecy was fulfilled upon the descendants of the priesthood, the people our enemies called today by the atonishment name, by the proverb name, and by the byword name "Haitians." Everything between the Levites and the other eleven tribes were cursed. Read that in **(Deutoronomy 28:16–20)**. The country name "Haiti" was the cursed name for the lineage of the Levites. The priesthood polluted the tabernacle of the congregation with unclean bread. In total, the Levites and the other eleven tribes were supposed to be the head of all nations upon the earth (Deut. 28:1). But because they despised the covenant, they became the tail among all the nations of the earth (Deut. 28:44). The reason why the lineage of the tribe of Levites and the other eleven tribes, who were the descendants of the slave, still survives is because of their fathers Abraham, Isaac, Jacob, and the covenant the Most High had with them after they left Egypt (Lev. 26:42–44). These were the only two reasons that still make them the elected of the Most High at the end of the heathen empire. The Most High will come, like the same way he came down to Egypt previously, to deliver us from the hands of our enemies.

Why did Haiti become a country with a cursed name for the lineage of Levites? Why could not the Haitians, since after their independence from France in 1804, make themselves together to rule? Why do they fight all the times? The answer is that the descendants of the priesthood are not supposed to have land to form a government, not supposed to sign treaties with the heathen nations. This is not what the Most High chosen them to do. Their jobs were to bring the word of the Most High to the other eleven tribes and bring their sins to the Most High. The job of the Levites were only in the tabernacle of the congregation, to keep those areas pure, because the Most High chose the Levites as a "firstborn" among the other eleven tribes. Read the real duty of the descendants of the priesthood who become the Haitians people today in 1 **(Chronicles 23:24–32)**. Their blessings changed in course. That's why they fight all the times in Haiti for power. The only way the descendants of the priesthood, the Haitians people and the other eleven tribes who are scattered among the heathens, could be delivered today. They had to return in the Torah to cure the wounds of their fathers and their own wounds, who were there several thousands of years. Read that in **(Leviticus 26:38–41)**. The Most High said the land of your enemies will eat you up. This prophecy was especially for the house of Levit, not the other tribes. Read that in 2 **(Kings 6:29)**, **(Leviticus 6:29)**, **(Ezekiel 5:10)**. In Haiti, the house of Levites, who became the cursed name "Haitians," their sons eat the flesh of their fathers, their daughters eat the flesh of their mothers, and their fathers eat the flesh of their daughters. In some areas in Haiti, the house of Levites changed dust into pancake and eat them. Read that in **(Ezekiel 5:8–9)**. This prophecy was not mentioned in the Book of Covenant. This prophecy again is for the house of Levi. In the **(Ezekiel 5:14–15)**, the house of Levi, in Haiti, become a "taunt" and a "reproach" before the eyes of all nations. Every time they fought between themselves for power, the other nations have to send a delegation in Haiti to unite them, because they couldn't put themselves together to do anything. The curse made them nuts. The Levites and the other eleven tribes were supposed to be in a position to help the other nations, but because they walked contrary to the Most High, the Most High walked contrary to them too. Now the Most High made the heathens in position to help them. The sons of Levites of who became Haitians today were supposed to be the priests

41

of the Most High. Now they became "enchanter," "witch," "charmer," "necromancer." The daughters of Levites who became Haitians today were also supposed to be pure before the Most High. Now they become "mambo." Read that in (**Deutoronomy 18:9–14**). The Most High said to the Levites, "I will change your cities in wilderness." Read that in (**Leviticus 26:31–32**). Look at Port-au-Prince. It became a waste, full with dungs, trashes, and ghosts. The whole land of Haiti became desolate; the enemies, meaning, the heathens who lived among the Haitians, the house of Levi in Haiti will watch the land of Haiti with an astonished eyes (32). Leviticus chapter 26 was only for the house of Levi, and Deuteronomy chapter 28 was also for the house of Levi, and the other eleven tribes. The country with a cursed name Moses announced on his prophecy, in the book of Leviticus chapter 26, was "Haiti." The Most High knew in the future, because of transgressions, the descendants of the priesthoods will have a land to rule, something they aren't supposed to be involved with. Moses told them, "Among you there will be no idols, no graven image, no standing image and no image of stone." Now if you look around the world, the descendants of the twelve tribes, who were scattered among all the heathens, they continue into the same transgressions, by helping the heathens worship all those idols under the umbrella of Christianity (Deut. 4:11–18). Now read verse 19. The Most High gave all those idols to the heathens to worship, but in verse 20, the "you" means the descendants of the twelve tribes. "You are my people, the sheep of my pasture." Read what Moses told them in verse 15. "The Most High has spoken to you, of the midst of the fire. You didn't see any face, watch onto your souls." Today the seed of the Woman, who become the nation of Israel, is scattered among the heathens, because of the transgressions of their forefathers and their owns transgressions. They helped the heathens worship the face of Julius Ceasar who died on March 15, 44 BC and was reborn on September 13, 1475, under the name of Cesare Borgia and became Jesus Christ (1490). There was one who was born in Nazareth, and there was one who was born in Rome. Among the two, which one does the whole world embrace today? Because the one who was born in Nazareth, Herod tried to destroyed him, because he was the seed of the Woman in **(Genesis 3:15)**. The other one came from the same seed with Herod (Gen. 3:15) Lucifer. It's very clear to see the answer. The whole world embraces the one who was born in Rome. The seed of the Woman who was scattered among the heathens worship the same idol, the same face Moses told their ancestors in (Deut. 4:15–18). "Be careful. Do not corrupt your souls with any idol." What the seed of the Woman refused to learn, what Moses told our ancestors, the same thing remain for us to follow today, but you have to be full of wisdom to understand which group of people among the heathens was the seed of the Woman in **(Genesis 3:15)**. The only way the seed of the Woman that became the nation of Israel will know who they are, each of them must ask themselves these questions.

1. We are the descendants of whom?
2. Shall we go forth?
3. What should we do to get out of this state?
4. What were the causes of our transgressions?
5. Why are we in this state today?
6. Why were our strengths exhausted so much that we could not free ourselves from the hands of our enemies?
7. If what we do is so wrong, who make us lose our identity as a nation?

The more you ask yourself those questions, the more you will do your own research (Deut. 13:14). Now pray to the Elohim of your forefathers to open your eyes, but you have to show him with all your heart, you want to know the truth, and he will open your eyes. Reading doesn't make you understand, if the Most High doesn't open your eyes. You will be able to accept and understand those hidden mysteries only if the Most High will give you the wisdom.

Warning

The Most High warned the seed of the Woman what will happen to them if they didn't keep the covenant. That was the only way you could be "wise" and have "understanding" (Deut. 4:6) and be the head of all nations (Deut. 28:1). But the seed of the Woman walked contrary and despised the covenant, and the Most High walked contrary to them and despised them too.

First, Moses told them, "If you despised the covenant, you will follow a group of nation in captivity. This group of nation carry out an Eagle for a symbol" (Deut. 28:49). Why did Moses use "a nation" in that verse? Because all are the same people, the heathens. All the heathens are the enemies of Israel (Ps. 83:1–9). The curse carry two elements, dispersion and captivity. The Book of Covenant mentioned more than five dozen verses about the enemy of Israel, more than one dozen verses about the dispersion of Israel, one dozen verses about the captivity, and more than one dozen verses concerning Israel, the seed of the Woman, who came from the twelve generations, who carry out the image, the likeness, and the royal blood of the Most High.

I never had any religious leader preached about these four elements—captivity, dispersion, enemy, and chosen people. Do you know why they don't preach that? If they preach that, they have to tell you which group of people among the heathens those verses talk about. They want you to know everybody in the whole earth carry the image, the likeness, and the royal of the Most High. That is the lie they want you to believe and continue to preach today. All the prophets from Moses to Malachi, they warned the chosen people about the consequence in case of disobedience to the covenant. "You will be scattered and in captivity in the hands of your enemies and even lose your heritage, your culture, your way of life," Read that **(Jeremiah 17:4)**.

But the chosen people refused to listen despite all the warnings from the prophets. The seed of the Woman still walks contrary to the covenant. After the Most High delivered them from Pharaoh in Egypt, after Joshua died, the seed of the Woman continued to follow the way of the heathen. Read that in **(Judges 2:11–12)**, specifically verse 19 (Judg. 3:7–8, Judg. 8:33–34, Judg. 10:6–7). Therefore, because of the Most High's anger against the chosen people, he sold them to six kings among the descendants of Ham. Here are the years of captivity (18+18+20+7+18+40=121 years in captivity). After, they left Egypt because of disobedience. If you read the whole Book of Covenant, from Genesis to Revelation, you will never read any verse about the Most High's anger against the heathen because they worshipped their deities. They didn't worship him. The Most High didn't expect the heathen to worship him, because he himself gave the heathen the things in creation. They could choose their deities. Read that in **(Deuteronomy 4:19)** and also read the difference the Most High established between his people and the heathens in **(Jeremiah 10:1–16)**. Despite the difference the Most High made between his people and the heathens, the chosen people still didn't recognize how the Most High loved them. They still continued their ways. More than dozen verses from the book of

Deuteronomy to Malachi explain the abominations and idolatry of the chosen people.

I encouraged all the descendants of the twelve tribes, who are among the heathen now, to read Ezekiel chapter 16. Each one of you who read that chapter will identify where the Elohim of your forefathers took you. Israel, you are the "chosen seed" before the foundation of the world (Eph. 1:4). Watch the word "elect" in that verse. It means you only "Israel." Any verse you read from Genesis to Revelation that interact with the word "elect" or "chosen," it means only you, Israel (precept upon precept Amos 3:1–2, Ephesians 1:4, and Ezekiel 16, but specially verse 8).

Watch the word "covenant" in that verse. Israel, all those words talk to you, because the whole book was the covenant between the Most High and you, Israel, detached yourself from the custom of the heathens. Come back to the creator of your forefathers, the Elohim of Abraham, Isaac, and Jacob. Read what the Most High said in **(Amos 5:23–24)**. "Take away from me the noise of your songs. These are the songs, you as a "chosen seed" sing among the heathens' religious organizations of the world. This is not what the Most High want for you as a "chosen seed." Read what he wants for you in verse 24. This is a mystery. The "chosen seed" had a difficulty understanding. Those prophecies were there for more than thousands of years. They were not even born. How come those words apply to them, but the way of the Most High is not your way. He knew all things before it happened. Read his way in **(Isaiah 46:9–10)**. He knew in advance you will disobey him. That's why his word came out from the mouths of his prophets against you, before you were even born.

Our ancestors asked Samuel for a king (1 Sam. 8:4–5). Samuel prayed the Most High and the Most High told Samuel to listen to the voice of them and establish a king over them (1 Sam. 8:22). Now the

Most High told Samuel to anoint Saul to be king over his people (1 Sam. 9:15–16). Saul was the first king who reigned over Israel's the twelve tribes, but things did not go well during the reign of Saul. The Most High rejected Saul and chose David to reign over his people. Why did Saul go astray? Why didn't any son of Saul reign after him? Because Saul didn't come from the tribes of Judah. If the lineage of Saul continued to reign, where will the "Shiloh" come, according to the prophecy of Jacob (Gen. 49:8–12). The Most High remembered the prophecy of Jacob, so Saul, who came from the lineage of Benjamin, must be replaced by David from the lineage of Judah to fulfill the prophecy of Jacob. Saul was the king the people asked, but Saul was not from the tribe Jacob mentioned on his prophecy, for the "Shiloh" to come from.

David reigned over all the twelve tribes of Israel for forty years (1 Kings 2:11), before he died, he told his son Solomon in verse (3) to keep the statutes, the commandments, the judgments. the testimonies of the Most High, something Salomon didn't do. Read 1 Kings 11:1–7) to see what Solomon did, before he died. Today did the chosen seed who was in captivity among the heathens do better than Solomon? The answer is no. They did the same thing Solomon did while several thousands ago, they helped the heathens worship their deities, and despised the statutes, the commandments, the judgments, the testimonies of Elohim of their forefathers Abraham, Isaac, and Jacob. During the (forty years) reign of King David, the chosen seed lived in peace. They did not go to any captivity to the other nations; however, read, one of the prophecies of king David in **(Psalm 137:3–4)**. Watch the word "captive." Why did King David speak about captivity? When the "chosen seed" lived in peace while he reigned. How did he know the chosen seed will be in captivity in the future? Let me show you where he knew that in **(Deuteronomy 28:64, 68)**. The same verse we read today in the Torah, he read the same verse also in his time. Before King David died, he transferred the royalty to Solomon, his son, because the "Sceptre" must not depart from Judah, until the "Shiloh" come, according to the prophecy of Jacob (Gen. 49:10). The "Sceptre" means the "royalty," the "kingship." Solomon reigned for forty years. Also, the chosen seed lived in peace while he reigned, but despite that, Solomon prayed the Most High for the "chosen seed." Read that in 1 **(Kings 8:44–53)**, specifically verse 53. Watch how Solomon called the people. The chosen seed will be in slavery among them his "enemies." How did Solomon know the chosen seed will be in captivity among his enemies? He red this prophecy in the Torah also, He knew it will happen in the future. Solomon, while he reigned, he didn't do well, before the eyes of the Most High. The Most High told him, because "You despised my covenant, I will rend the kingdom from you, but I will not do it while your life, because of David my servants, and for Jerusalem my city, I will rend it, from the hands of your son (1 Kings 11:11–13). And after all, Solomon slept; his son Rehoboam reigned in his place (1 Kings 11:41–43).

After Solomon slept, the Most High divided the kingdom, in two parts, as he said to Solomon before he died. Rehoboam, his son, reigned over two and half tribes, in the south, and Jeroboam, son of Nebath, reigned over nine and half tribes, in the north. Read that in 1 **(Kings 12:1–33)**, but specifically verses 28–31 to see the crime of Jeroboam. He made two calves of gold, then he said to the northern tribes, "This is your deity, who brought you out of Egypt." Why did Jeroboam do that? Because he didn't understand the biblical prophecy, he didn't not know why the Most High divided the twelve tribes in two kingdoms. Perhaps he read the Torah, but ignored it, or he didn't read it at all. Watch Solomon. He read the Torah, according to his prayer, for the "chosen seed" in the book of 1 **(Kings 8:44–53)**, but still he committed encroachment against the Most High. Maybe that was the case for Jeroboam. Because, if he read the Torah and practiced what he read, he would have known what Jacob said to Joseph about Ephraim and Manasseh, in **(Genesis 48:5)**. Why didn't he recognize them like Reuben and Simeon? Because Jacob knew, in the future, his house will be into the hands of Ephraim (Ezek. 37:19–22).

According to verse 19, Joseph was supposed to be the head of the northern tribes, but because Joseph will not be there during the time of the division of the kingdom and Ephraim will not be there also, but Joseph had a double honor among the other eleven tribes. His son's name became the head of the northern tribes. Any verse you read in Hosea about Ephraim, it means the house of Israel. If the kingdom wasn't divided, how would **(Genesis 48:5)** be fulfilled, because the Most High knew why Jacob adopted Ephraim and Manasseh. Each of them had something to do among the twelve tribes, but Jeroboam did not understand the mystery I'm explaining to you now. Maybe he thought the kingdom was divided because of his tactic, without paying attention about what the Torah said several thousands years before. The chosen seed who was in captivity, among the heathens today made the same mistake Jeroboam made before. They refused to come back to the Torah for the transgressions of their forefathers and their owns transgressions; instead, they still continue to help the heathens worship the same calves of gold Jeroboam made several thousand years before. They even refused to accept they are the chosen seed according to prophecy. Read what prophet Isaiah said about them in **(Isaiah 1:2–4)**. Watch the word "ox" and the word "ass" in verse 3. These two animals knew their masters. It means they are better than the chosen seed. Most of them who read this prophecy today refuse to accept the prophet talk to them. They thought those prophecies had nothing to do with them. Read the reason the chosen seed refused to listen to the words of the prophets in **(Ezekiel 3:7)**. According to this verse, they refused to listen to the Most High, the hard heart their descendants had several thousand years ago. Today they had the same hard heart, like saying the proverb "like father like son."

Jeroboam was the first king for the northern kingdom. He did evil in the sight of the Most High (1 Kings 12:28–31). Hoshea was the last king of the northern kingdom. He did evil also in the sight of the Most High (2 Kings 17:1–2). The Most High said enough is enough. Now he will fulfill part of the prophecy. He told Moses in **(Deutoronomy 28:64)**, around 721 BC, Shalmaneser, king of Assyria, invaded Samaria., He brought captive all the nine and half tribes. Read that in 2 **(Kings 17:6)**. Since that time, the stick of Joseph, who was into the hands of Ephraim, was in captivity among the heathens, despite all the warnings from Moses in the Torah about what will happen to them if they despised the covenant. This stiff-neck people never listened until today. They remained the same people as before among the heathens. They were married with the heathen customs, because of transgressions. Read the way they become among these nations (Deut. 28:65–67). This cruel situation pushed them to think in their hearts. They became a dried bones (Ezek. 37:11) without breath into their nostrils. In total, read the whole chapter of **(Ezekiel 37)**. Those prophecies weren't fulfilled yet. The lineage of the Woman in **(Genesis 3:15)**, who was in captivity among the heathen today, when they read this chapter, they don't know if the chapter spoke to them. Why? Because they refused to show the Most High in their hearts. They want to know the truth; therefore, the Most High despised them also, but those who show the Most High today they want to abandon the heathen custom and return to the covenant, he opened their eyes, He let them know who they are.

One part of **(Deutoronomy 28:64)** was fulfilled around 721 BC, upon the head of the northern kingdom. The other part remained to be fulfilled around AD 70, upon the head of the southern kingdom, because the southern kingdom will go astray also. The southern kingdom wasn't better than the northern kingdom, but the southern kingdom must remain in Jerusalem, until "Shiloh" came (Gen. 49:10). The word "Shiloh" means the "Messiah." The descendants of King David must continued the lineage of king, until the "Shiloh" come, because, he must come into the root of David. So the southern kingdom remained in Jerusalem for 651 years. Rehoboam, the first king of the southern kingdom (1 Kings 12:1), prepared his army to fight against the house of Israel, to bring them back under his domination, but the Most High said to Shemaiah, "Go and tell Rehoboam, don't make war with the northern kingdom. The division of the two kingdoms came from me." Zedekiah was the last king of the southern kingdom. He did evil in the sight of the Most High (2 Kings 24:18–20). Zedekiah replaced his nephew Jeconiah. Now during the reign of Zedekiah, Nebuchadnetzar, king of Chaldeen, invaded Jerusalem and brought the house of Judah, the house of Benjamin, and half the house of Levi into captivity in Chaldee for seventy years (Jer. 25:11–12). Why did I avoid saying the word "Babylon" or Ne-buchadnetzar, king of Babylon? Let me tell you the reason.

Many people who read the Book of Covenant thought Babylon only apply to the Chaldeen empire. The answer is no. Babylon was a biblical name for all the heathens empires, beginning with Chaldeen empire, to the United States of America, the last world empire. The unclean spirit who controlled those empires was Lucifer. For example, you will never find the word "United States" in the Book of Covenant, but any verse you read in the book of Isaiah or the book of Jeremiah about the daughter of Babylon, that was a reference to all European empires, including United States of America. The book of Revelation referred to those empires as Babylon, the Great. Nebuchadnetzar also made a reference to "Babylon the Great" (Dan. 4:30) but not for his time, because the old Babylon wasn't powerful like the new Babylon now. The old Babylon didn't have the weapons the new Babylon have now. All those empires are the enemies of the chosen seed. They must come from the place they are and manifest in public and go to perdition before the kingdom of the chosen people is established forever in the whole earth. The Most High did not reject his chosen seed at all, but because of transgressions, he let the heathen punish us. After we complete the numbers of years for numbers of transgressions we have committed, he will take us from the four corners of the earth, He will forgive us, purify us, and bring us back to our mother for breastfeeding. After that, he will bless us and multiply us more than before. Because we don't have the same mother with the heathen, the mother of the heathen was Semiramis, queen of the heavens (Jer. 44:18–19). Our ancestors, the chosen seed, worship her also. Today the chosen seed who was in captivity among the heathen worship her too. The Most High sent his servants, his prophets to our ancestors, against this mystery Woman (Jer. 44:4–5). Read what they said to Jeremiah (Jer. 44:15–17). Today the chosen seed did the same thing. The Most High sent his servants to them to let them know they are the "chosen seed." They refused to listen. They still continued to worship those deities. The Most High defended their ancestors to worship. Now at the end of time, the new Babylon called her the Lady of Liberty. Each country worships her under different name—for example in Greece, Aphrodite; in Egypt, Isis; in Rome, Venus; in India, Kali; in Canaan, Ishtar; in America, Lady of liberty. The French made her statue, like she's pregnant with her son Tammuz, with the torch of Nimrod, his husband into her hand. Nimrod was the sun god or sun dog. The Egyptian deity dog head god. Semiramis is the moon god. History changed the deity dog head god of the Egyptians, so the word "god" or "dog" came from to those masquerades. So the queen of heaven you read in (**Jeremiah 44:18–19**) is right there in front of your eyes, in New York, under the name of "Lady of Liberty." Nimrod is the king of Babylon; Semiramis is the queen of Babylon.

The southern kingdom remained in Chaldee for seventy years, because Manasseh, during his reign, did evil in the sight of the Most High (2 Kings 21:1–18). He didn't walk the same way his father Hezekiah walked with the Most High. Watch what the Most High told Jeremiah: "Even if Moses and Samuel came before me, I will not forgive Judah" (Jer. 15:1–9), specifically verse 4, so Judah must go to Chaldee to pay for all the abominations Manasseh committed in Jerusalem during his reign. Watch the way the Most High will clean Jerusalem. Read that verse in 2 **(Kings 21:13–14)**. The word "line" in verse 13, and the word "plummet" in the same verse mean the number years of punishments of the southern kingdom in the Chaldeen empire will be equal to the number of violation of the northern kingdom in Samaria and the house of Ahab. Because if you added the age of Manasseh and the number of years he reigned, you get 67 (55+12=67) years, but 67 wasn't a prophetic number. It must be rounded up to 70. The book of Leviticus gave us the formula for all commandments the chosen people violated. Remember the Most High gave his commandments only to the house of Jacob. The Most High didn't make any covenant with other nations. Read that for yourself in **(Psalm 147:19–20)**. Apostle Paul repeated the same thing in **(Romans 9:4–5)** (Ps. 147:19–20 precept upon precept Rom. 9:4–5). All provisions in the book of the covenant were only for house of Jacob. Religious organizations around the world preached the Most High created all men with the same blood. That is a big lie. Compare **(Acts 17:26 with Ezra 9:2)**. If all men were created with the same blood, Ezra has no reason to call that a sin; therefore, **(Acts 17:26)** wasn't in line with **(Ezra 9:2)**. The tabernacle of Edom just added **(Acts 17:26)** to put everybody, including themselves, among the chosen seed. Read what the Most High told the "chosen people" in **(Exodus 19:6)**. In that verse, read those expressions a kingdom of priests and "a holy nation." It means the "chosen people" must be pure in spirit, in blood, in flesh, and in word compared to the heathen. Read also what Nehemiah said on his book (Neh.13:23–31) specifically verse 25. Those verses are not in line with **(Acts 17:26)**. Those words on Acts 17:26 are not the words of the disciples or the apostles, because they knew the truth. Read what Peter said in **(Acts 5:29–32)**, specifically in verse 30. Peter didn't say, the Most High of all, but the Most High of our fathers. In verse 31 also, he didn't say the word "repentance" and the word "forgiveness" attributed to everybody, but to the "house of Jacob" only, but even if I make it clear for you to understand, this is not my job to open your eyes. You have to show the Most High with all your heart you want to know the truth, then he will open your eyes to make you understand this mystery. Now let's come back to the captivity of the southern kingdom by Nebuchadnetzar. Judah has to be in Chaldeen empire for seventy weeks, meaning seventy years (Dan. 9:24). According to the formula of the Torah, within seventy years, a lot of things happened to the Chaldeen empire, the Most High drove out Nebuchadnetzar into his kingdom (Dan. 4:25, 30, 33). In verses 36–37, it seems like Nebuchadnetzar repented before the Most High and returned to his kingdom, but that wasn't the case. His son Belshazzar reigned in his place, and Belshazzar himself forgot what happened to his father. Read what he did in **(Daniel 5:2–4)** while he enjoyed his wine. Read what he saw in verses 26–28 on the wall of his room after Daniel gave him the significance of these three words. Read what Darius the Median did to him in verses 30–31 in the same night. Darius himself followed the same way with Nebuchadnetzar and Belshazzar. Read what he did in **(Daniel 6:7)**. Everyone of his kingdom must pray to him, but Daniel refused to do that (13). Read what he did to Daniel in verse 16, but he didn't do it with all his heart. He did it to satisfy his people. Read what, he said to Daniel in the last part of the verse. Read what Alexander the Great did to Darius in 332 BC. The ram in verse 4 was Darius; the goat in verse 5 was Alexander the Great. Read what the ram did to the goat in verse 7, since that time, the Babylonian system was transferred from the Chaldeen empire to Greco-Macedonian empire. All those things happened within the seventy years of captivity of Judah. After the first seventy years (Dan. 9:24), Judah returned to Jerusalem.

Now in **(Daniel 9:25–27)**, there are seventy more years, but something is missing here. You have to read the book of first Maccabees and the book of second Maccabees to understand what happened within seventy-three years after Alexander replaced Darius as a Chaldeen king. Even if Judah returned to Jerusalem, they were still under the control of the Greek. Alexander reigned for years and died (1 Mac. 1:7). His kingdom was divided among four generals of his clan (9). Read that also in Daniel 8:8, while the reign of those generals came a wicked man among them who was called Antiochus, surnamed Epiphanes. The Roman kept his father (Antiochus). The king was hostaged in Rome. The little "horn" you read in **(Daniel 8:9)** was Antiochus Epiphanes, the wicked. Read what he did to the chosen people in verses 10–12. The seven weeks in **(Daniel 9:25)** equal seven years. The sixty-two weeks equal sixty-two years, but according to the formula of the Torah, something is missing here. The sixty-two weeks must round up to sixty-three weeks (63+7=70) weeks. The half weeks in verse 27 equal three years so (70+3=73 years). It seems like the translator of the book of Daniel does not give us too much information about this prophecy. In **(Daniel 9:24)**, 70 years; **(Daniel 9:25)**, 70 years; and **(Daniel 9:27)**, 3 years equal 143 years between the time of Daniel and Malachi. There was no king in Jerusalem during that time. The chosen people were under the control of the high priest. **(Daniel 9:27)** told us about the wicked man, but didn't tell us what he did. Read what he did to the chosen people in 1 (**Mac. 1:20, 39–44**), during his seventy-three years of reign, but one day while he was on way to go to Jerusalem to prosecute the chosen people, the Most High smote him with an incurable and invisible plague. Read that in 2 (**Maccabees 9:9–13**). The last part of (**Daniel 9:27**) was the plague of the wicked Greek man (Antiochus Epiphanes). The worms rose out of his body, his flesh fell away, his smell was noisome to all his army. He himself couldn't abide his own smell. In total, the house of Jacob must read the first and second book of Maccabees to see what the Greek—the children of Esau mixed up with the children of Japheth—did to their ancestors (1 Mac. 5:3, 9). That's why, the tabernacle of Edom took away those books in the Book of Convenant, because they didn't want you to read about it. They didn't want you to know who you are.

Where Are the Descendants of Esau Now?

It seems like the house of Esau vanished away from the planet. Why have we never heard someone say, "I came from the house of Esau?" Everybody on earth now does not want to be a descendant of Esau. Why? Let me turn the question around: who wants to be the lineage of Cain? Nobody. Let me tell you the reason. There was a big mystery behind that. Why did the Most High hate Esau before he was even born? Because the evil spirit who entered the garment called Esau was the same evil spirit who was in the garment called Cain. Esau was born to continue the lineage of Cain, who was destroyed during the flood. Jacob was born to replace Abel, who died without living the posterity. Lucifer tried to stop the Most High's providence, by pushing his son Cain to kill Abel, but no one can stop the Most High's providence. It will happen the way he wants it to happen. Read **(Genesis 5:1–32)**. You won't see Cain among the sons of man, because he wasn't the son of Adam. He was the son of Lucifer. Read **(Matthew 1:1–17)**. You won't see Esau among the sons of man, because, he wasn't the son of Isaac. He was the son of Lucifer also. This is the big secret religious organizations don't preach to their members. In **(Genesis 25:25)**, Esau came out a red man. The reason why? The Book of Covenant mentioned his color.

This was the first man who was born like that since Adam, but Jacob came out pure in color. The Book of Covenant didn't say anything about which color he came out. It seems like the stamp the Most High put upon Cain (Gen. 4:15) was to put out the red color upon Esau, when he was born. Look upon yourself. You will see this mystery. Under the brown color was the red color. Why did Esau (Gen. 25:33) swear and trade his birthright with Jacob for a red soup (34)? Remember in verse 25, Esau was born a red man. Why did the pastors and the evangelists who preach now never revealed the mystery behind Jacob and Esau? Read the reason, in **(Amos 3:7)**. They were not the servants of the Most High. The Most High revealed his secret to his servants. The Most High revealed to me the secret between the two men. The brown color symbolized humility; the red color symbolized pride. The humility covered the pride. (Jacob was the son of man who was born with humble nature. Esau was the son of Lucifer who was born with pride). Even Esau knew he already sold his birthright with Jacob for the red soup, he knew Jacob did nothing wrong, he refused to humble himself. The pride in him made him think he will wait for the last day of his father to kill Jacob.

In **(Genesis 4:14)**, Cain used "wandering" and the word "vagabond" for himself, after the Most High told him his punishment for killing his brother Abel. In **(Genesis 27:40)**, Isaac told Esau to "wander here and there" to avoid being a slave to his brother. "Wandering" and "vagabond" means the same thing. With "wandering here and there," there is no doubt, the birth of Esau was the second apparition of Cain, one spirit used two different garments. Now from that red soup came out his biblical name "Edom." The house of Esau has eleven dukes (Gen. 36:40–43). Today which group of people uses the word "duke" among them? The Europeans. Why hasn't one European country called themselves "duke"? Remember the prophecy of Isaac upon Esau. In

(Genesis 27:40), the descendants of Esau must wander here and there among other people, trying to hide themselves. That's why today, you will never find any single country that lives by the house of Esau only, but they are "wandering here and there" among the house of Japheth, the house of Gehazi. Remember, according to the curse, the prophet Elisha put upon Gehazi, the Hebrew. His descendants remained white albinos forever (2 Kings 5:27). In total, the descendants of Japheth, Gehazi, Kenites, and the Canaanites formed today remarkable Gentile nations, in Europe, part of Asia, United States, Canada, Argentina, and the Promised Land. Why didn't I mention Esau? Because the descendants of Esau was supposed to be a "wandering people" among them, but they are very powerful people on earth now. According to the prophecy of **(Obediah. 3:4)**, he described what, he saw as a nest, because the word "science and technology" were not there yet. He tried to tell us about the "space program" who was controlled by the descendants of Esau in Europe and America. The house of Esau controlled all banks, all precious metals, all maritime, all governments, and the stocks markets in the world today. Read verse 3 to see how high their habitations. Obediah tried to tell us about the high-rise buildings around Europe and America. The last part of verse 3 said, "Who shall bring me down to the ground?" Today in the mouth of which group of people, you heard the same familiar expression? By saying "too big to fail" in the mouth of the Europeans' and the Americans' power. It means for them the "IMF" and the "world bank" were too big to go to the ground. According to the last part of verse 3, the prophet told us how much wealth the house of Esau will accumulate in the last day. But nothing is too big before the Most High to go the ground. When your day comes, all the prophecies in the book of Obadiah were mostly about the rise and fall of the house of Esau. The problem of the house of Esau is that they refused to humble themselves. They want to be always in the high position. They want people to bow down before them. When the Book of Covenant spoke about the tabernacles of Edom, in **(Psalm 83:6)**, this verse referred us, to Vatican who was mostly controlled by the house of Esau. Vatican is the tabernacle of Edom. In total, the house of Esau controlled all religious organizations in the world now.

After the seed of the Woman left Egypt, they met face-to-face with the seed of the Lucifer, in Rephidim, the descendants of Amalek. Who was Amalek? He was the son of Eliphaz (Gen. 36:12), the grandson of Esau. This is the first war between the seed of the Woman and the seed of Lucifer (Ex.17:8–16). In verse 14, read what Moses was told to do. Was the seed of Amalek completely destroyed in that war? The answer is no. The Most High took a decision. In the future, he will completely erase the seed of Amalek under the heaven. I heard a lot of rumors today saying the descendants of Amalek are still among the heathen, but what people didn't understand, the Most High never take his word back. Let's look in the Book of Covenant to see if we will not find any verse that say the seed of the Amalek was completely erased under the heavens. Why did Moses avoid to call the seed of Amalek Edom? Because his seed won't be under the heavens, until the end of time. The other sons of Eliphaz and the sons of Reuel carried the biblical name Edom, until the end of time. Let's continue to see what happened to the descendants of Amalek.

In **(Judges 7:12–25)**, there was a war between the seed of the Woman and the Madianites. There were some Amalekites in that war. All of them were destroyed. There was a war again between the seed of the Woman and the seed of Lucifer in the book of 1 **(Samuel 14:47)**. The word "Edom" on that verse means the other sons of Eliphaz, son of Esau, and the sons of Reuel, son of Esau, but not Amalek, the seed of Ammon, the Zobah, and the Philistines, They were born according to the flesh. They did not carry biblical names. Only Jacob and Esau carried biblical names, because Jacob was the seed of the Woman, and Esau was the seed of Lucifer the ancient Serpent,in verse (48) the prophet separated Amalekites with the other sons of Esau, because the descendants of Amalek just waited for their destructions. Let's continue. In 1 **(Samuel 15:6–9)**, read those verses. You won't see the word "Edom" there. Why? Because the other sons of Eliphaz and Reuel were not among them. Saul told the Kenites to depart among them. In that war, Saul almost destroyed all the Amalekites and took Agag, the king, alive. Let's continue again in 1 **(Samuel 27:8)**. There were some Amalekites among the Geshurites and the Gezrites in that war. David destroyed some Amalekites who lived among those nations. Finally, read what happened to the rest of the Amalekites in 1 **(Chronicles 4:42–43)**. Verse 43 shows us clearly the seed of Amalek was completely erased under the heaven. What the Most High told Moses in **(Exodus 17:14)**, he did it in 1 **(Chronicles 4:42–43)**, precept upon precept.

The other sons of Esau, Eliphaz, and Reuel—their sons carried the biblical name "Edom"—were there for a certain period of time. Why? Remember the prophecy of Isaac in **(Genesis 27:40)**? The house of Esau must not only wander here and there among other heathen nations, but they must wander here and there among other heathen nations with a new name. Let me tell you a secret. Why do religious organizations never tell their members which house the Herods came from? If the verse they're reading mentioned Herods, they just said Herods but never told the members which group of people the Herods were from. Why? Because they came from the house with the Herods they knew the truth, because if they didn't know the truth, they won't be able to hide it. Members of all religious organizations in the world were controlled by the house of Esau today. There are certain things they don't want you to know. Let me show you something for example in **(Matthew 2:1)**, the verse mentioned Herod. In the book of **(Malachi 1:4)**, this verse mentioned Edom. This Herod-Edom called himself Herod the Great. Yahusha was born during the reign of this Herod. **(Luke 1:5)** spoke about the same Herod. Another example, in the book of **(Acts 12:1)**, the verse mentioned again Herod. **(Number 24:18)** mentioned Edom. This Herod-Edom was Herod Agrippa 1. **(Acts 12:1)** mentioned the word "church." It was a lie. During that time, there was no church in Jerusalem, during the reign of the Herodians dynasties. In the place of the "church" they supposed to put the house of Judah, at that time the full house of Jacob, wasn't in Jerusalem. There were only three tribes in Jerusalem Judah, Levite, and Benjamin. They put "church" in that verse to make think there was a church in Jerusalem. In that time like Baptist, Seven Days Adventist, and Pentecostal church (ect.), there was only the clan of Pharisees who were controlled by rod the Edomite and the clan of Scribes who were controlled by the house of Recab. While the reign of Herod Edom Judah, Benjamin and Levite lived in the same territory, with the house of Esau., But they were not occupied any position, the Herod Edom was in charge of everything. They ruled Jerusalem, for more than 150 years, but under the control of Rome. Let me show you another place in the Book of Covenant, the translator put their own word to fit their agenda, for example Matthew 16:18, in that verse Yahusha never mentioned the word church because there was no word church in the Torah, He said something about the house of Jacob, but the translator put in that the word church. When you read, that will make you imagine. He spoke about the Gentiles' church in Europe or everywhere else, in the world, the word rock he used in that verse referred to himself, not Apostle Peter. Compare **(Matthew 6:18)** with **(Matthew 21:42)**. You will see exactly the truth. He tried to tell the disciples, the house of Jacob was built upon him, according to the formula of the Torah, not the Gentile churches.

Let's talk little about the house of Rechab, means the Rechabites people who were with the seed of the Woman since the time of Moses. This group of people came from the house of Kenite (Judg. 1:16). The verse said the children of Kenite, Moses's father-in-law, but don't mix up them, with the Kenians people today. This Kenite name was the name of one man who came from the same family member with Reuel, father-in-law of Moses, because (Judges 4:11) said Heber the Kenite distanced himself from the other Kenites, the sons of Hobab, the father-in-law of Moses, but in **(Exudos 2:16–18)**, the father-in-law of Moses was called Reuel and had seven daughters. The Book of Covenant didn't say if Reuel had sons also. Where did these people come from? But one thing for sure, they came from the house of Reuel, the Medianites, and descendants of Ishmael. They were among the seed of the Woman as clerks, secretaries, or writers, because in the book of 1 **(Chronicles 2:54–5)**, they described them as scribes they were many scribes among the priestwood of Israel also. For example, **(Ezra 7:6)** describes Ezra as a scribe, meaning, clerk, secretary, and reader. The difference, the Rechabite scribes were not allowed to be among the priesthood scribes, because they were not from the house of Jacob. After a certain period of time, the house of Kenite changed name. It became the house of Rechab. That's why, 1 **(Chronicles 2:55)** mentions the city of Hemath, where the father of Rechab came from. In **(Jeremiah 35:2–6)**, the Most High told Jeremiah to bring the house of Rechab to his house, to drink wine, the Most High already knew what the house of Rechab will say to Jeremiah., But he used the house of Rechab as example, to show the seed of the Woman how they obeyed their forefathers' voice. Now read the answer of the house of Rechab to **(Jeremiah in verses 6–11)**. Read what the Most High told Judah in verse 14. How the house of Rechab listened to the voice of Jonadab, their fathers, but me I spoke unto you mourning, but you refused to hear my voice. In verse 17 the Most High said he will punish Judah with all evils he pronounced against them, but read verse 19 to see what, he said about the descendants of Jonadab, son of Rechab.

Between the book of Matthew to the book of Luke, we had several verses about the clan of the scribes that was the same group of people in Jeremiah 35, the only difference is they didn't mention the house of Rechab no more. They lived in Jerusalem for a long period of time with Judah and the house of Esau, the Edomite Herod, the house of Rechab, and the house of Esau detached with Judah around AD 70, when Judah went to slavery. Until today, why do both houses call themselves Juif or Jewis today? The Most High revealed to me the mystery, the house of Rechab, called Juif or Jewish, came from the house of Kenite or Hobab, the Medianites people who came from the house of Ishmael the son of Abraham. Read in **(Judges 1:16)**, to see how long they lived with the tribe of Judah. They were more familiar with the tribe of Judah than any other tribe. That's why the word Juif or Jewish were more important for them than the word Israel. After a long period of time, they detached themselves from the word "scribe." They established the clan Judaism, together the Rechabites and the Edomites, and another group that came from the house of Ashkenaz, the son of Gomer, the grandson of Japheth joined them (Gen 10:3). Today instead of calling themselves different name from their forefather's houses, together they call themselves Juif, all around Europe, United States, Israel, and Canada. But you won't find them too much in the West Indians countries and Africa. There are two clans of them, Judaism and non-Judaism. The Judaism dressed in black at all times, together with the orthodox who dressed in black dress. But the non-Judaism dress like everybody else. Why won't you find this clan of people who dress in black in Africa or the West Indian countries? There's a reason for that. Read the reason in the book of (**Zechariah 6:1–8**), especially verse 6, when Zechariah has the vision of four chariots. He was in Jerusalem. The north of Jerusalem was Europe. The black horse and the white horse went in the same direction. Many preachers who read the Book of Covenant don't understand this mystery, but the Most High revealed that to me. The black horses symbolized the Orthodox Church and the Judaism Juif who were always dressed in black. The black horses typify the uniforms, the white horses symbolized the Roman Catholic Church that was always in white dress. Why did those horses leave from south to north? Because those people who established those organizations in Europe came from Jerusalem or other countries not far from Jerusalem. The speckled horses remained in the country not far from Jerusalem in the south. The speckled horses symbolized Islam, Muslim, and Buddhism. Those organizations carried many different garments, with many different colors, speckled red, black and white garments. The four chariots are the same, meaning with the four winds. They symbolized four unclean spirits who are behind those groups. Those spirits help them expand the false doctrine all over the world, because from those groups came out the Christianity doctrine. The devil used those groups to deceive the whole world (Rev. 12:9). The horses on (**Zechariah 6:1–8**) didn't have the same meaning with the horses on (**Revelation 6:1–8**). The horses on (**Revelation 6:1–8**) symbolize wars, sword, famine, noisome beast, and pestilence, specifically verse 8. Contagious disease like AIDS, swine flu, diabetes, cancer, and more. All that is part of the blood, because the Most High created man with pure blood, but the pure blood was infected in the Garden of Eden, because Lucifer, the ancient Serpent, mix up his blood with the pure blood. That's why today, we experience all those diseases in the blood stream. If you go to any hospital today, you will see all the nurses and the doctors with gloves in their hands before they even touch any patient, but without thinking the mystery of this infection. This is not something the human science can see. Only the Most High knows what kind of germ Lucifer injected into the pure blood. No doctor in the whole world can cure this disease. Only the Most High can take out this germ into the pure blood. Read what he will do for the house of Jacob only. Before he bring them back to the promised land, in the book of **(Ezekiel 36:22–27)**, specifically verse 25 that tell us what kind of medicament the Most High will use a clean water but nobody know what kind of water it is. Only He knows what kind of medicament it is. That the only medicament who can take out the germ out of the pure blood. The pale horse in **(Revelation 6:8)** symbolizes the secret crafty counsel. The seed of Lucifer will take to destroy the seed of the Woman, with all king the diseases. Remember the seed of Lucifer now controls all branches of government in the world. According to the book of Obadiah, verse 3, the house of Esau will be extremely rich at the end-time, but after all, the house of Esau will sit in the ground, without throne, without dignity. Read that in **(Isaiah 47:1)**. Why do I know the prophet spoke about the new Babylon when the same verse said "O virgin daughter of Babylon" because the verse said also "O daughter of the Chaldeans"? Four great empires, with ten horns, must use the Babylonian system. The first one was the Chaldean empire who was the mother of the system. The second was the same empire, but under Medepersian rule. The third was the Greek empire, under Alexander the Great. The fourth was the Roman empire with the ten horns. When the prophet said "O daughter of the Chaldean," he didn't talk about any country. But about the same system. The other three great empires with the ten horns will use as Chaldean empire. In that case, Chaldean empire wasn't the mother of the country, but the mother of the system. This is the system Lucifer used to rule the world, and over the seed of Woman, but this system is almost at the heel of the house of Esau, because the end of the house of Esau will be the beginning of the house Jacob to rule this world forever. Now my last chapter will be about the son of the Most High. Why did the Most High send his son, to have flesh garment like the other brothers from the seed of the Woman?

Who Was Yahusha

Was Yahusha born in the physical world? The answer is no. The physical world only duplicated what already happened in the invisible world. Yahusha was the son of the Woman in **(Genesis 3:15)**, and Myriam was the mother of the garment. Yahusha was the one among the seed of the Woman. The Most High told Lucifer he will bruise your head and also your seed will bruise his heel. This prophecy took several thousands of years before accomplishment. The mystery of who was the seed of Lucifer the Most High told Lucifer who will bruise Yahusha heel. Religious organizations in the world never revealed this mystery. They read **(Genesis 3:15)**, but they didn't understand it, because the Most High didn't reveal who was the seed of Lucifer in **(Genesis.3:15)**. Who will bruise the heel of Yahusha? The Romans, who delivered Yahusha to be crucified. Pilate who was the seed the Most High told Lucifer who, among his seed, will bruise the heel of his son. Read that in **(Matthew 27:26–38)**, specially verse 26. Precept upon precept, compare **(Matthew 27:26)** with **(Genesis 3:15)**. Even Pilate washed his hands (verse 24). It doesn't mean anything. He delivered him to the soldiers anyway. On that day, the truth that came out from the mouth of Yahusha made two seeds of Lucifer became friends again,

Herod and Pilate (Luke 23:12). Both came from the house of Esau. Sometimes the same thing happened today among us. If three men met together and had three different opinions, the one who told the truth will be victimized by the two others, even if they were incompatible in opinion also. They will become friends to fight the one who told the truth. It means the truth can destroy the wall of the two enemies and make them friends again. Now let's read what Moses said about Yahusha in **(Deutoronomy 18:15–19)**. In those verses, try to understand the way Moses talk. His conversation does not covert everybody in the world but only the house of Jacob. He will not only be a prophet, but a brother for them, meaning, the same bloodline, What mystery is that? Today when the seed of the Woman who was in slavery among the heathen read those verses, they don't understand if Moses spoke to them. Why? Because the transgressions of their forefathers and their own transgressions make them forget who they are. Moses not only talked to the brothers of the house of Jacob who were with him in that time. He spoke to you too, the rest of the house of Jacob who are among the heathen in slavery today. The covenant was between the house of Jacob and the Most High. It wasn't for all nations. The apostles, in their time, understood what Moses said. Read that in **(Acts 3:22–26)**, but today, the rest of the seed of the Woman, who associate themselves with the heathen in pagan worship, do not understand if the scripture talk to them. When they read it, it seems like what they read have nothing to do with them. O, Israel, return to your creator. That's the only way we can be free from our enemies. O, Israel, Jesus Christ wasn't your creator. Jesus Christ was the god of your enemies. If you look inside the name of Julius Caesar, you will find the pagan name Jesus Christ. Do you think the name of the son of the Most High will be very close to the name of the son of Lucifer? The answer is no. Let's take a closer look at the name of the Most High and his son. According what he told Moses

72

in the book of **(Exodus 3:14–15)**: "I am that, I am it means the way I was, the way I will always be no change on me. What I said, I said it forever." In Hebrew, "Ahayeh Asher Ahayeh." The Hebrew language gave two translations for the son's name Yeshua. Yahusha was the same name, very close to the father's name. The Christians' organizations don't pray in those names. They pray in the name of Jesus Christ, the deity of the Greco-Roman empire, because the Greco-Roman empire was the father of the Christianity.

Let's take a closer look to see how many gods the Greek worship: Zeus, Poseidon, Hermes, Hera, Hades, Dionysus, Apollo, Demeter, Ares, Artemis, Athena, and Aphrodite. In total the Greek worship twelve gods. Now let's take a closer look to see how many gods the Roman worship: Jupiter, Juno, Neptune, Pluto, Apollo, Diana, Mars, Venus, Cupid, Mercury, Minerva, Ceres, Proserpine, Vulcan, Bacchus, Saturn, Vesta, Janus, Uranus, Gaia, Maia, Gordon, and Cerberus. In total, the Roman worship twenty-three gods. Members of Christianity worship all those gods, because the Romans and the Greeks come from the house of Esau and Japheth. The Most High don't make any covenant with those houses. If anybody calls the Most High god, that means you don't have any respect for the creator, because you put the Almighty in the same range with those masquerades.

Let's now take a closer look at the aspect of Yeshua, according to the book of **(Isaiah 53:1–12)**, especially verse 2. He has no desire in him to satisfy the sinner world, according to those verses. We read in Isaiah 53, he was not handsome physically and yet from him, all things were created. Read that in **(Colosians 1:16)**. He also carried the image of his father (verse 15). What caused him to come into a garment, nobody could digest. He also said, "ask the fish, ask the birds." We can even talk to the earth. The earth and all those animals could teach us about the perfection and the beauty of the creation. Read it in **(Job 12:7–10)**.

What about for himself, because verse 2 on Isaiah 53 said, he has no desire on him to make somebody love him. Not only did he carry all the sins of the house of Jacob upon him, he also wanted to teach the house of Jacob a lesson. Read that in the book of **(John 6:63)**. He said the flesh profiteth nothing. All the words he said came from the Spirit, meaning the invisible world. He remained connected with his father. He tried to teach the house of Jacob not to worry about the physical body, whatever it was, ugly or handsome, but to make sure the man who talk inside the garment was pure. This is the meaning of beauty, because what we consider as beauty is different from what the divine family consider as beauty. Observe what is right and do what is right. This is the real meaning of beauty for the divine family.

Yahusha was born during the time of silence, meaning the Maccabeens' time, between the book of Malachi and Matthew, must of Hebrew Isralites returned to Jerusalem after Alexander the Great with one horn destroyed the two horns of Daruis, but not all. The houses of Judah, Benjamin, and Levite were in slavery into the Chaldeen empire. When Daniel was into the den of lions, under the Daruis's rule (Dan. 6:16), one day while Habakkuk prepared his dinner, the angel of the Most High told Habakkuk, "Go, carry that dinner to Daniel, who was in the lions' den in Babylon." Habakkuk said to the angel, "I never knew Babylon and I didn't know where the den is." The angel of the Most High took him by his spirit and set him in Babylon where the den was. Daniel arose and ate, and the angel of the Most High took Habakkuk the same way and brought him back to Jerusalem immediately. But you won't read this mystery in the book of Habakkuk. You will read it in **(Daniel 14:33–39)**, in the Septuagint, becaue the rest of the book of Daniel chapter 13 and 14 were in the Septuagint. The rest of the prophets from Hosea to Zechariah accomplished their missions while Daruis was still king of the Chaldeen empire. I encourage the seed of the Woman today to read **(Daniel 13,14)**. The thirteenth chapter is about a remarkable Hebrew woman named Suzanna, who accepted to die, instead of lying before the Most High. The fourteenth chapter is about the controversy between Daniel and Daruis. Daruis wanted Daniel to worship his idols. Daniel refused him and answered that only the Elohim of Israel who created the heaven and earth deserved to be worshiped. This is the same idol Daniel refused to worship. You, the seed of the Woman who came out from the same house with Daniel, helped the heathen worship today in Christian organizations, while during the times of Daruis, this organization was called pagan, while during the Greco-Roman empire, this organization was called Christianity—nothing new under the sun.

You, the seed of the Woman who was among the heathen in slavery today, read the prayer of Daniel for the house of Jacob in **(Daniel 9:7–13)**. When you read verse 7, Daniel knew the northern kingdom was already among the heathen in slavery since the time of Hoshea, king of Israel. In his prayer, he talked about the captivity of Judah into Jerusalem and the captivity of Israel in Samaria, because Daniel knew very well the Torah (verse 13). He called the five books of Moses the Law of Moses. Daniel knew after seventy years in Babylon, Judah will return to Jerusalem to wait for the coming of the Shilo to accomplish what Jacob said in **(Genesis 49:10)**. Read what the Shilo said before he left to his father in (Luke 21:24). It means Judah will return to slavery again until today. Therefore, in the prayer of Daniel, all the "us" and the "we" are attributed to the seeds of the Woman alive today among the heathen. The Shilo did the same prayer in **(John 17:1–25)**, especially in verse 9. He made a difference between the house of Jacob and the heathen. He said, "I pray for them," meaning the house of Jacob. I pray not for the world, meaning the heathen. Yahusha and Daniel knew they had to be in line according to the formula of the Torah.

Religious organizations in the world today read those prayers. They think Yahusha and Daniel prayed for everybody in the world, because they do not understand the formula of the Torah (Jn. 17:1–25 precept for Dan. 9:7–13).

Why did Herod the Great want to kill the son of Miriam? If you don't understand the formula of the Torah, you won't understand the mystery behind that. Herod knew the mystery behind that, because he read the Torah., He knew what the Most High told Abraham, Isaac, and Jacob, in the book of Genesis. He knew the seed who will possess the inheritance of the whole earth will come from Jacob, not Esau, his forefather. He knew something religious organizations in the world today don't know. Read what happened to him in **(Matthew 2:1–3)**. He had the news the king of Israel was born (verse 3). He was troubled. Why? Because for him, the last king of Judah was Zedekiah who came from the house of Jacob (Jeremiah 52). For him, after several years have passed, there was no king from the house of Jacob, the seed of the Woman. For him the only way he will continue to rule that land and his descendants after him is to kill that king, who came from the house Jacob, because, if he didn't kill him, he will be in trouble. He and his descendants will be out of the land, because he didn't inherit the land he ruled. He knew that because he knew the scripture very well. The dynasty of Herod ruled the holy land for more than 150 years. They were Edomite from Genesis to Malachi. After that, the Edomite biblical name changed for Herod's biblical name after a certain period of time. The Herod changed for European. This is the same group of people who ruled the world with the Babylonian system since 332 BC. Today the word "great" is the only word to identify where the house of Esau is. Which group of people used to call themselves great? Around 374 BC, the house of Esau, the Herods, the descendants of the same family emigrate to the land the prophet Joel called before the land of

Greece (Joel 3:6). Another translation called it the land of Javan, one of the sons of Japheth. I will explain the prophecy of **(Joel 3:6)**, at the later time. Now let's focus on the word "great." Nothing new under the sun today in the mouth of which group of people you heard the word "great" is from the mouth of the Europeans. This is the sign that show us where the house of Esau is. They always want to be great, since the time of the dynasty of Herod.

Let's take a closer look at some of the things Yeshua did or said while on his mission with the disciples, because religious organizations who read the Book of Covenant mix up what he said about the house of Jacob and what he said about other nations. He won't say anything about who was not in line with the Torah. He knew the law of Moses very well. For example, what he said in **(Matthew10:28)** referred only to the house of Jacob, because he knew the war between the seed of the Woman and the seed of Lucifer. **(Genesis 3:15)** will proceed until the end time. Read another example in **(Matthew 15:24 and 26)**. In verse 24, he referred to the house of Jacob, and yet in verse 26, he referred to other nations. The language he used for the house of Jacob and the language he used for the heathen were very important to understand those mysteries. Another example, in **(Matthew 25:33)**, in the first paragraph, who did he call the sheep? The house of Jacob. Read that in **(Ezra 34:12–13)**. In the second paragraph who did he call the goats? The heathen. Read that in **(Daniel 8:5–8)**. To understand those mysteries, precept must be upon precept, line upon line, here a little and there a little (Isa. 28:10). In **(John 8:43)**, many religious leaders in the world who read that verse thought Yeshua only spoke to the Pharisees while on his mission on earth. The answer is no. He spoke to you too, who is afraid of the truth, the same way the Pharisees were afraid of the truth, because religious leaders in the world today don't understand the language of the son of the Most High. They have the same heart as the

Pharisees and the Sadduces. Religious leaders today read those verses too, in **(Matthew 13:10–17)** but do not understand the language of those verses. In verse 11, the "you" refers to the disciples who came from the house of Jacob. Verse 12, the first paragraph was for the disciples who came from the root of Abraham; the second paragraph was for the heathens who didn't have or know nothing about the mystery of the kingdom. The truth that came from Yeshua even took away what they had, because if you're the enemy of the truth, when you hear it, it destroys everything you already have. Verses 13–15 are for the heathens. Why? He spoke in parables in verse 13 and explained why in verses 14–15. Read the answer in **(Matthew 7:6)**. Who did he call dogs and who did he call swine in that verse? The heathens who lived in the same land with the house of Jacob. He didn't want them to hear the mystery of the kingdom he brought from the father for the house of Jacob, because they will do with those holy things what he told you in **(Matthew 7:6)**. Now come back to verses 16–17, from **(Matthew 13)**. All the "your" in verse 16 and all the "you" in verse 17 referred to the disciples who came from the house of Jacob. Among the Sadducees, Pharisees, and the Scribes, there were some Hebrew Israelites also, but because they were afraid of Herod Antipas I, they despised their own brother Yeshua.

Yeshua must be completely perfect in physical body, invisible in body and in blood, among all the descendants of the twelve tribes. Let's take a closer look at the mystery of the feast of the Passover. After the sin, the color of "Heylale" changed from brown to red. Read that in **(Revelation 12:3)**. He was a red man. Cain and Esau had the same color as him. The Most High didn't create him with the red color. So Yeshua was the only one among the seed of the Woman, his body and his blood can wash the whole house of Jacob, put the infection away from them, and bring them back to the original state before the sin. Read what he said to the disciples at the time of the Passover. In **(Mark 14:22–25)**, in verse 22, take "eat this, this is my body." In verse 24, the translator is supposed to write the first paragraph like "this is my blood, the blood of the covenant," but he put it this way, "this is my blood of the new testament." That's wrong. There is no new covenant yet. The Most High will make a new covenant with the house of Jacob. Read that in **(Hebrews 8:7–13)**. Why? Verse 8 mentions two houses, because the northern kingdom was in exile in Africa, including the Middle East countries. The southern kingdom was in slavery in Europe and America. Read that in **(Isaiah 11:11–12)**. Before the Most High will make a new covenant with them, he will put the two houses together. Read that in **(Ezra 37:19)**. Those prophecies weren't fulfilled yet.

Now let's go back to the last paragraph of **(Mark14:24)** that says, "Which is shed for many." Does that mean everybody in the world is included? The answer is no. Which group of people did Moses sprinkle the blood of the covenant over? The house of Jacob only (Ex. 24:8). "Which is shed for many" means all children of Jacob that are near and that are far off, in slavery among the heathens. This is the meaning of the Passover. Only Yeshua can deliver the whole house of Jacob from the ancient dragon. Read his fight with Satan for his people in **(Matthew 4:1–11)**. Satan has no problem with the other nations. His only problem was the seed of the Woman in **(Genesis 3:15)**.

People who read the Book of Covenant today or people in the time of Yeshua didn't really understand the mystery why Yeshua gave himself, in sacrifice for the house of Jacob, because they didn't understand the scripture. Yeshua didn't come to fight with human beings. He was in war with Lucifer the Serpent of **(Genesis 3:15)**. Yeshua knew the scripture very well. For example, in **(Matthew 27:11)**, who asked

Yeshua this question: "Are you are the king of the Jews?" those words came from the mouth of Pilate, but Yeshua knew very well Satan asked him this question, not Pilate. In verse 12, Yeshua didn't say anything to people who accused him because he wasn't in war with them. In verse 13, Satan asked him a question again. In verse 14, he didn't answer anything. Even Pilate said in verse 23, "What evil hath he done?" Even he washed his hands in verse 24. Even Judas Iscariot repented in verse 3. All those things do not mean nothing. Pilate and Judas Iscariot were the sons of Lucifer. They had to do their father's walk. People who read the scripture todaydon't understand the invisible sense of it. When you read **(Matthew 27:11–14 and Mark 14:53–65)**, Lucifer arrogantly asked the son of the Most High those questions, according to **(Genesis 3:15)**. He knew one day, he will face one of the seed of the Woman. He did not know which one of them, but when Miriam gave birth to Yeshua, now he knew who it was. Then he moved his son (Herod the Great) quickly to destroy him.

Yeshua was resurrected in the same body. Read the reason in **(Mark 10:33–34)**. In verse 33, those scribes and those priests who considered themselves Jews, most of them were Gentiles, Edomites, and Rechabites. In the last paragraph of the same verse, few of them were Hebrew Israelites. Verse 34 explains why. Yeshua was resurrected in the same body to show the disciples what he told them before, and he showed them also, in **(Mark 16:14)**, while they sat together without knocking on the door, he showed up among them. But before he couldn't do that, because he had the sin of the house of Israel upon him, but after the resurrection, his father gave him his glory back, because he was without sin. He didn't need to die to leave his physical body and enter it again. He tried to show the house of Jacob, how they will be in the kingdom. This privilege was only for the house of Israel. It wasn't for everybody in the world, like religious organizations preach today. The strangers will be among the seed of the Woman when the kingdom of Israel is established upon earth, like slave and servants. Some heathen countries who didn't have the seed of the Woman among them as slave will servants; some heathen countries who had the seed of the Woman among them as slave will be in slavery too among the seed of the Woman (Isa.14:1–2).

Happiness Awaits Israel

Let's take a closer look at the immigration, when the kingdom of Israel is established upon the earth. Let me show you something about the strangers in the Book of Covenant, because, sometimes, the word "strangers" is used between Israel and Israel and Israel and the heathens. For example, in **(Number 1:51)**, the word "stranger" in this verse means the other eleven tribes. The tabernacle was under the responsibility of the Levites, and yet, in **(Exodus 23:9)**, the word "stranger" in this verse means the heathens who were among the twelve tribes. Let me show another way, when two different verses used the word "stranger" and both verses mean the same thing. For example, in **(Isaiah 56:3)** and **(James 1:1)**, both verses mean the same thing—the descendants of the twelve tribes who were in slavery among the heathens. Isaiah used the word "stranger" and James used the word "scattered." Read in 2 **(Kings 2:17–18)** to see how Solomon used the immigrants who were among the twelve tribes. He gave them work. He did not send them back to their countries, because he knew what the Torah said about the "strangers." Now people of the earth didn't know anything about the Elohim of Abraham, Isaac, and Jacob. When will they fear him? When the kingdom of Israel is established upon the earth. Read what

Solomon said about that in 1 **(Kings 8:41–43)**. The word "strangers" in those verses means the other heathen nations. People will come far off to go to Jerusalem to pray the Elohim of Israel. Solomon asked the Most High to hear them. Let me show you another way Apostle Paul called the Israelites who were born in the heathen country in **(Galatians 2:2–3)**. In verse 2, he said he preached to the Gentiles. Which group of people did he call Gentiles in that verse? The Israelites who were born in Greece in verse 3. He called Titus Greek, because Titus was an Israelite who was born in Greece.

Let's read **(Galatians 3:28–29)**. In verse 28, he said, "Neither Jew nor Greek. The word "Jew" he used in that verse means an Israelite who was born in Jerusalem, and the word "Greek" he used in the same verse means an Israelite who was born in Greece. In verse 29, he said, "If you are in Yeshua"—meaning the same house, the same family with Yeahua—"you are Abraham, the seed." The word "seed" he used in that verse means the same bloodline. He does not mean brother in Christ the way religious organizations preach it today. When Paul said he preached to the Romans, the Corinthians, the Galatians, the Ephesians, the Philippians, the Colossians, the Thessalonians, he didn't mean the heathens, but the (Israelites) who were born among the heathens nations, he called those Israelites the citizens of those nations. Yeshua established Paul to preach to those Israelites who were scattered among the heathens since the time of Hoshea, king of the northern kingdom. People who read the Book of Covenant today don't understand the language of the apostles. They thought the apostles preached to the heathens. Read what Paul said in **(Acts 26:22)**. The last paragraph said, "Saying none other things than those which the prophets and Moses did say should come." He remained (precept upon precept) line upon line with the formula of the Torah. This is the language the apostles used to talk about the immigration of the Israelites among the other heathen nations. For example, an Israelite who was born in Greece was a "stranger" to an Israelite who was born in France. Why? Because the Most High scattered them among all the heathens (Deut. 28:64). Any verse you read in the Book of Covenant, if the verse mentioned the word "stranger," pay attention to this word until you understand if the verse used that word among the twelve tribes, if the verse used that word for the twelve tribes among the heathens, or if the verse used that word for the heathens among the twelve tribes. In the Book of Covenant, the word "stranger" does not mean the heathens only. Sometimes, it means the house of Israel. According to prophecy, the house of Israel will be among the heathens until the end of time of the governance of Esau. After that the table will turn.

Let's see what will happen when the table turns for Jacob, how the immigration will be when the Most High returns the governance of the earth to the hands of the seed of the Woman, because the seed of the Woman did slave on all heathens empires. They ruled their governments with investigative judgment. Many god heads and the "Dragon" and his seed were the ruler of the earth. The immigration law was different between countries. Some country send people back to the country where they came from. But when the table turns for the seed of the Woman, the dragon and his seed won't play any role in that government. Let's read 1 **(Corinthians 2:6–9)**. In verse 6, Paul speaks about perfect "wisdom," a wisdom anybody in this world experiences. In verse 7, Paul said this wisdom is a mystery. In verse 8, Paul said if anybody in this world knows that wisdom, they won't crucify Yeshua. Paul said in verse 9 what he said in verses 6–8. It is things the eye never saw, ear never heard, will never enter into the heart of man. The last paragraph say those things are for the love one of the Most High. The problem is that, if you don't understand the language of Paul in the last paragraph, you may think Paul said the Most High loves everybody in the world. Let's reveal the precept that will make us understand which group of people Paul referred to in the last paragraph. Which group of people did the Most High offer this wisdom to before? The house of Jacob Compare 1 **(Corinthians 2:6–9)** with **(Deutoronomy 4:6)**. This is the group of people Paul referred to, in the last paragraph of verse 9. Which group of people the Most High love? Compare 1 **(Corinthians 2:6–9 with Amos 3:1–2)**. The love of the Most High was for the house of Jacob, the seed of the Woman from **(Genesis 3:15)**. The seed of the Woman will rule the kingdom of the Most High, with those precious elements you read in 1 **(Corinthians 2:6–9)**, Now you understand the language of Paul in the last paragraph.

Let's see how the immigration will be, in this powerful kingdom. This kingdom will be controlled by power and Spirit. Read that in 1 **(Corinthians 4:20)**. Why did Yeshua say, in **(Luke 17:21)**, you can't see this kingdom, and yet this kingdom is within you? It will be controlled by the invisible power. In this kingdom, you won't need airplanes, ships, cars, and other mechanical things to travel country to country. Let's see how the house of Jacob, who will rule that kingdom, will travel. Read that in **(Luke 24:36–39)**. In verse 36, he showed the disciples how the transportation will be. In verse 37, the disciples were afraid of what they have seen, because they have never seen some kind of transportation like that before. In verse 38, Yeshua saw the disciples were terrified and troubled, because, he showed up among them in Spirit. After that, the Spirit entered his garment among them. The Spirit told the disciples, in verse 39, "Touch my hands and feet. It is me. The house of Israel will rule this kingdom with this kind of body.The other nations will depend on that kingdom to survive." Today, everybody wants to come to the United States to work. The promised land will be much more powerful than the United States when the Most High puts the two kingdoms together to rule the earth forever. Other nations will go to the Promised

Land to bow before the house of Jacob. Read that in **(Isaiah 60:10–12)**. During that time, a nation that refuses to go to the Promised Land to serve the house of Jacob should perish (12). In verse 5, the abundance of the sea will be ready for the house of Jacob—meaning, the wealth under the sea, a fortune, the human being will never be able to touch now. The Most High preserved them for the house of Jacob, who was in slavery among the heathens today. In the last paragraph in verse 10, he said to the house of Jacob, "For in my wrath I smote you, but in my favour have I had mercy on you." Those prophecies were not fulfilled yet. Israel, wake up. This book will help you understand the Book of Covenant. Because this covenant was written by your ancestors, try to understand how the Elohim of your ancestors loves you. According to the prophecy of **(Zechariah 8:22–23)**, the immigration office will be full of strangers, all of them will go to pray the Elohim of Abraham, Isaac, and Jacob. According to verse 23, some of them will be in need of all things. They will go to seek some help from the house of Jacob. They will have some form of immigration paper—visas or residence permit—the same way the heathen nations did it today.We are very close to the end, because the house of Esau is almost at his heel so that the house of Jacob will start using his hands.

Now, if you go fishing in the international sea in Europe, you won't catch any fish in the coast of Scandinavia, Scotland, Mediterranean, and North Atlantic Sea. The only things you will catch are nuclear-powered attack submarines. These are the fishes you will catch under the sea of Europe now. More than 150 submarines travel on those areas twenty-four hours a day, all of them full with nuclear missiles. Each of this missile carries six, eight, or ten warheads, enough to obliterate the whole earth. Nobody knows what happen to the heathens. Let me tell you the secret. You harvest what you sowed. Before the heathens were united together. They destroyed the house of Jacob, servant of the Most

High (Ps. 83:1–8). All the heathens were on those verses. Now that curse followed the heathens from Baal, Nimrod, to the United Stated of America, the last heathen empire. Those submarines aren't for the country who sent them under the sea. They are for the Most High. Those officers who worked inside those submarines are working for the Most High. The country who possesses those weapons are even afraid of them. Why are you afraid of what your hands made? Read the reason in 2 **(Edras.16:12–16)**. In those verses, you will see those weapons are not for the country who made. They are for the Most High. Some of those weapons will be shot by a terrible earthquake, because the foundation of the earth will be shaken, the sea level will rise from the deep (12). In verse 13, the Most High will shot those missiles from one end of the world to the other. No one can extinguish this fire. In verse 16, Esdras described the payload who will unleash this missile as an archer. When the missile is unleashed from this archer, it won't come back to its base anymore. Those weapons will be unleashed at the time the Most High desires to use them to punish the heathens for what they did to house of Jacob.

Let's see how the Most High will protect the house of Jacob before he unleashes the three woes in **(Revelation 8:13)**. Now let's see how he protects the house of Jacob before when they were in Egypt, because precept must be upon precept. Let's read in **(Exodus 12:21–23)**. In verse 21, Moses told the elders of Israel to prepare for the Passover. In verse 22, the Most High told them to "strike the lintel and the two side posts with the blood." It means all the houses in Egypt where the children of Israel lived have a blood mark. Let's see at the end of time where that "mark" will be upon the children of Israel. In **(Revelation 7:3–8)**, the word that will make us understand which group of people John talked about is the word "servants" in verse (3). Which group of people did the Most High call his servants before? Let's read in **(Leviticus 25:42)**. In verse 42, the whole house of Jacob, in verses 4–8, John told us the whole house of Jacob will receive a "mark" (Lev. 25:42, precept for Rev.7:3). When you compare the "code servants" in both verses, that will make you understand which group of people John referred to in that chapter. Now that "mark" won't be in the front door where the children of Israel lived. It will be in the foreheads of all houses of Jacob. Before there were twelve tribes. Now there were twelve thousands. It means twelve was a perfect number for the house of Jacob. Twelve thousands of each tribe means the whole house of each tribe, without children and women. When John says twelve thousands of each tribe, it means twelve thousand men prepared for war. Always remember the house of Jacob was an army for the Most High. Let's focus now on the first woe.

The first woe in **(Revelation 9:1–12)**, but specifically 7–10, we need to understand the nature of this mysterious locusts. Did the Most High use that locusts before? The answer is yes, but there are few details about the one the Most High used before Moses. This is the same locusts. Why did John give more detail? Because at the end of time, those locusts have a different work to do. They must be armed with new weapon. The first time the Most High punished the Egyptians with those locusts, they turned the land of Egypt like a desert. They ate every herb, all the fruit of the trees. There was nothing left for the Egyptians. Read that in **(Exodus 10:12–15)**. It seems in verse 16, Pharaoh repented, but it means nothing for the Most High. Read what Paul says about Pharaoh in **(Romans 9:17)**. Paul quoted Moses in **(Exodus 9:16)**. It was a terrible plague for Pharaoh. The Most High will use the same locusts (Rev. 9:1–12) in verse (4). They will not hurt the nature because of the last paragraph: "but only those men which not have the seal of the Most High in the foreheads." John gave a different description of them because they won't do the same work like they did before. Now they will bite men for five months during which there will be no death of anyone. The Most High will keep death away for five months. That's why. Each one of the whole house of Jacob received a "mark" in **(Revelation 7:3–8)**. The mark was to protect them from the bite of the locusts (Rev. 9:6). Men will seek death, but there will be no death. The locusts will not be there to kill, but to torment men day and night for five months. In those days, the darkness will cover the earth. The locusts will cover everything, inside and outside all houses. Read the description of those locusts between verses 7–10. Compare **(Revelation 9:7–10)** with **(Exodus 10:12–15)** (precept upon precept). This is the same locusts, but different work to do. On those days, the house of Jacob will be in peace. They will only observe the suffering of the heathens. There will be no need to go to the hospital, because doctors couldn't help on those days. Their houses will be filled with locusts, the whole world will be in darkness, there will be no help nowhere in the world. This is the time to punish this world. This is the first woe.

Now let's take a close look at the second woe (Rev. 9:13–21). In verse 14, the angel referred to the great river (Euphrates). This river was the boundary of the Promised Land in the northeast part. The Mediterranean Sea was in the northwest part of Damascus. The four angels in verse 15 will start the clean up in the northeast part of the Promised Land and go all around the boundary to the southwest, northwest, southeast, and kill all the heathens who are now the only people who remain alive in the land the Most High promised to Abraham, Isaac, and Jacob. After those plagues, even the people who received the mark (Rev. 7:3–8) saw what those plagues did (Rev. 9:20), they still continued to worship demons and idols. The verse did say if those men were heathens who live inside or outside the Promised Land. In verse 14, the four angels means four men also. Six men means six angels did that job already, in the Promised Land, but not upon the heathens. They did it upon the rebellious people from the house of

Jacob. Read that in **(Ezra 9:1–11)**, but they received order from the Most High in verse 4 not to touch anyone from the house of Jacob who got a mark in the foreheads. In verse 6, the Most High told them to begin in his sanctuary (Rev. 9:18). Their weapons will be fire, smoke, and brimstone, and in **(Ezra 9:2)**, they were called instruments of destruction. They were the same group of men, but with different weapons and different work to do. **(Revelation 9:14)** mentioned the great river Euphrates, and **(Ezra 9:2)** also mentioned the six men were in the north part of the Promised Land (precept upon precept).

Now let's take a closer look at the second woe in **(Revelation 10:1–11)**. What will be fulfilled in this chapter was very important for the house of Jacob. In verse 1, John spoke about an invisible personage that was the same personage Ezekiel spoke about in **(Ezra 1:26–28)**. The translator identified him as an angel. If you compare **(Revelation 1:1)** with **(Ezra 1:26–28 and also Revelation 1:14–15)**. According to those verses, this personage is none other than Yeshua in verse 2. Which book was on his hands? The Torah, the five books of Moses. In verse 3, who were the seven thunders? The seven thunders were seven angels. In verse 4, John was about to write what the seven thunders said when another voice told him not to write what the seven thunders said. If anybody says he knows what the seven thunders said, he's just lying to you. Nobody knows until today what the seven thunders said. The words of the seven thunders mean seven other books that weren't opened yet. Those words were sealed until Yeshua will come again among his brethren, the house of Jacob. Verse 7 is the most fascinating verse in the Book of Covenant. This verse tells us about the whole mystery, who will be fulfilled at the end of time. If anybody said they understand this verse, if you don't identify in that verse, what you waiting for has already passed. You just don't understand it. This verse brings you back to the scriptures of the servants of the Most High, the prophets, and the voice of the seven angels. All the mysteries the Most High told the prophets about the house of Jacob will be fulfilled. It means what you are waiting for is not the New Testaments. Religious organizations like to read, but not the scriptures of the prophets, from Moses to Malachi, because the New Testaments were duplicates from the scriptures of the prophets. In verse 10, John took the little book from the hands of the angel and ate it up. It means the contents of the Torah was "sweet as honey in his mouth." The words of the Most High was very sweet in the mouth of the people. Read that in **(Psalm 19:8–11)**, but the practice is not easy for some people. Let's come back to **(Revelation 10:10)**. Why was John filled with pain after eating the little book? The pain symbolized the iniquity of the house of Jacob.

Chapter 11 of Revelation is a continuation of chapter 10 verse 2. In that verse, the angel told John not to measure the outside of the temple. The word "temple" doesn't mean a building. It means the rest of the house of Jacob, who was among the Gentiles. There will be under the feet of the Gentiles for 42 months, 30 days equal 1260 years, since the year of AD 70, the holy city was under the feet of the Gentiles until today. Read in 1 **(Corinthians 6:19)**. You will see what the angel means by the word "temple." All the "you" or the "your" in that verse are attributed to the house of Jacob. That's why he told John there was no need to count them now, because they will be among the Gentiles for some time. The word of the angel in **(Revelation 11:2)** was the same with Yeshua in **(Luke 21:24)**. The last part of the verse, when the rest of the house of Jacob will be back at the Promised Land at the end of time. According to the prophecy of Daniel, the end of time will start within the times of 1260 years (Dan. 12:7), but when did those years start? It started with Roman empire, but not with the BC dictators or kings, but with one of the AD emperors. According to the prophecy of Daniel again (Dan.7:25), who changed the law of the Most High to the "grace" the Christianity preached today? The Roman empire. Who made the house of Jacob forget the original Hebrew calendar today and follow the heathen's calendar? The Roman empire. In that times, the power of the holy people will be completely broken. Read that in **(Daniel 12:7)**. The last part of the verse (Dan. 7:12) spoke about an extention of times, but the verse didn't say how many years the extention of times will be from those empires from the (AD) emperors to the United States of America. In verse 3, from Revelation chapter 11, who were the two witnesses? In verse 6 who shut the heaven that it rained not in the days of their prophecy? Elijah. Read that in 1 **(Kings 17:1)**. Who changed water to blood? Moses. Read that in **(Exodus 7:19)**. The Most High chose two big miracles that happened to his two servants, to represent his chosen people among the heathens. In verse 7, the dragon killed the testimony of the law and the words of the prophets from the mouth of the chosen seed. Verse 8 spoke about corpses, but in verse 9, they didn't put them in the graves. If somebody is physically dead, if they lived that body, in the street, he won't be there for long. Who was this group of people that left their dead in the street of Babylon means the European and the American continent, without putting them in the graves for 1260 years? The rest of the house of Jacob, why didn't they put them in the graves? Because they're not physically dead. They were considered as dead people, because the of law the Most High gave to Moses for them and the words the Most High gave to the prophets for them were dead in the mouth of the chosen seed (9–10) while the times of 1260 years, because the words of the Most High died in their mouth. The heathens rejoiced. They sent gifts to each of them, but verse 11 says, after the 1260 years, the Spirit of the Most High entered them, and they woken and stood up on their feet. Now, how do we know the 1260 years were over? Because many Hebrew Israelites now know who they are. Many of them received the Spirit of the Most High from European

93

and American continent, but many of them who were in Christianity, the European religion refused to accept they are the chosen seed. The Book of Covenant says they still remain the dead people in the street of Babylon. The last part of verse 11 says, when the heathens saw the dead people, they knew who they are and heard the words that came out from their mouths. They were not the same with Christianity. They're afraid, in verse 12, the Most High will protect his chosen seed before the earthquake on verse 13. The word "heaven" in verse 12 doesn't mean the Most High will take them to another planet. It means, "move from one place to another" on earth (precept upon precept, Rev. 11:1–14 with Ez. 37:1–28). Those prophecies were fulfilled today.

Let's take a closer look upon the third woe. What will happen in earth when you read **(Revelation 11:15)**? Remember, I said before, the table will turn, so in verse 15, the table turns. The kingdom of the house of Esau was replaced by the kingdom of the house of Jacob. The last part of the verse says "this kingdom will reign for ever and ever." This is the mystery announced before by the prophets. Compare **(Revelation 11:15 with Daniel 7:18)** (precept upon precept). You will see what I told you. It is the government or a universal moment established here. The heathens fell under the power of the house of Jacob (16–17). We don't have too much description about the (twenty-four elders), but divinely, they were angels. Quote Yeshua in **(Matthew 22:30)**. The last part of the verse, in verse 18, the heathens will feel betrayed when that happened, but they can do nothing. In verse 19, the word "temple" means the house of Jacob. Read about the temple in **(Revelation 21:9–26)**. The Ark of Covenant will be among the house of Jacob again. The last part of the verse says there will a power deployment in that times— lightnings, voices, thunders, earthquake, and a great hail. Let see among the seed of the woman who will not heir the kingdom, if they fell into that category. Let's read 1 **(Corinthians 6:8–11)**. In verse

9 fornicators, idolaters, adulterers, effeminate, and abusers; in verse 10 thieves, covetous, drunkards, revilers, and extortioners; in verse 11, Paul told them, some of them lived their life like that. In those verses, Paul didn't speak to the heathens, but to the house of Jacob. The heathens can live like that if they want, because the Most High didn't give them any law to follow (Ps.147:19–20), but you as a chosen people, be careful of those things. If anyone of you had those things in your life, you will not inherit the kingdom.

Conclusion

Now Israel, my brethren, tell me, which group of nation upon earth is happy like you? You can't compare yourself with any nation on earth. You are the people of the Most High, him who created all things. Eyes can see or cannot see. Israel, read what the Most High did for our ancestors after they left Egypt in (**Deuteronomy 4:37–38**). Because he loved our forefathers and still loves us today, he drove out nations to give their land to our forefathers. Which god of other nations did that for them? None of them. Now we are in the last days called Jacob's trouble. Read that in Jeremiah 30:7, but our father was rest assured that trouble is not for him, but for his descendants, who were among the heathens today. There was no trouble between Lucifer and the heathens. Lucifer was at war with the seed of the Woman since the beginning until today. That's why the end of time is called Jacob's trouble. We are the remnant seed of the woman (Rev. 12:17) who will confront Lucifer for the last time. Many of us will perish because of the commandment of the Most High and the testimony of Yeshua. The Most High was very patient with us. He wanted us to come back to our pasture, but, Israel, one day his patience will be over. We don't know that day, but he knows it. Everyone among us who refuses to repent for the last time will face destruction, because, after the slavery in Europe and America, there will be no other place to send us to slavery for disobedience.

How did our ancestors come to Europe and America? In slavery. Read that in **(Deutoronomy 28:68)**. The word "Egypt" in that verse does not mean the country of Egypt. It means "a place you will work as a slave." Read the same prophecy in **(Joel 3:6–7)**.

Remember I said before I will be back to this prophecy. Why did Joel use the word "Javan" or "Grecians" in this verse? Because those areas were occupied by the house of Japheth, Esau, Gehazi. Dan was a judge among them. According to the prophecy of Joel, in the future, the house of Jacob will be into the hands of those houses in slavery, in Europe and America. In **(Luke 21:24)**, Yeshua renewed the same thing, in the year 70 AD. Part of this prophecy fulfilled the year the last part was fulfilled. In the middle of 1492 to 1500, the house of Ham joined with the house of Ishmael and the house of Lot. They sold the house of Jacob to the house of Japheth, Esau, Gehazi, and Dan, who became Europeans, at a later time.

We are the descendants of this group of people we call today the "slave trade." In French, "la traite des esclaves." Israel, we have two signs in the Book of Covenant that show us we are the true descendants of Abraham. Let me show you the first sign: because Joseph arrived in Egypt as a slave, Pharaoh changed his name. Read that in **(Genesis 41:45)**. The second, in Chaldeen empire, Nebuchadnezzar changed the names of our ancestors. Read that in **(Daniel 1:7)**. When our ancestors arrived in Europe and America as slaves, the slave master changed their names. The sign followed us from Egypt to Europe and America.

For example, my last name is Bacourt. The master gave to my forefather his last name, in the time of slavery. My forefather worked for the French master in an industrial pottery in the north of Haiti. Today the French (white Bacourt family) still lives in France.

Israel, read 1 **(Kings 8:22–53 and Dan. 9:3–19)** and prayer of Yeshua (Jn. 17:1–25). Those prayers are for you alive today. Israel, this is the prayers of your ancestors.

May the Most High richly bless you after reading this book, and come back to your pasture.

"That will be a big day, when the two kingdoms joined together (Ezek.37:19), Ephraim will not envy Judah, meaning the northern and the southern kingdoms (Isa.11:13), they will sing together (Isaiah the twelve chapter), they will weep together, for all transgressions they committed among the heathens while the times of the captivity (Jer.31:9). That day will be the day of deliverance, the "Most High" will take them from the land of their enemies, and bring them back, to the promise land, their mourning change into joy".

Printed in the United States
By Bookmasters